The Data
Asset

Wiley & SAS Business Series

The Wiley & SAS Business Series presents books that help senior-level managers with their critical management decisions.

Titles in the Wiley and SAS Business Series include:

For more information on any of the above titles, please visit **www.wiley.com**.

The Data Asset

How Smart Companies
Govern Their Data for
Business Success

TONY FISHER

WILEY

John Wiley & Sons, Inc.

Published by John Wiley & Sons, Inc., Hoboken, New Jersey.
Published simultaneously in Canada.

For general information on our other products and services, or technical support, please contact our Customer Care Department within the United States at 800-762-2974, outside the United States at 317-572-3993 or fax 317-572-4002.

Wiley also publishes its books in a variety of electronic formats. Some content that appears in print may not be available in electronic books.

For more information about Wiley products, visit our Web site at http://www.wiley.com.

Library of Congress Cataloging-in-Publication Data:

Fisher, Tony (Anthony), 1958-
  The data asset : govern your data for business success / Tony Fisher.
      p. cm.—(Wiley & SAS business series)
  Includes index.
  ISBN 978-0-470-46226-3 (cloth)
  1. Database management. 2. Business intelligence. 3. Corporate governance. I. Title.
  QA76.9.D3F58 2009
  005.74—dc22

                                                            2009010884

Printed in the United States of America

10 9 8 7 6 5 4 3 2

Contents

Fore! word

No, this is not a book about golf, but knowing the author as I do, I can confidently state that golf and data quality are two driving forces of his life. Data quality is a great deal like golf—only the truly experienced understand the complexity. Fortunately for all of us, Tony Fisher has unparalleled experience that he is willing to share.

Unfortunately, in some organizations, data quality and data governance seem to have taken a back seat to enterprise projects involving business intelligence and data warehousing. One of the main reasons for this situation is that data governance requires coordination and communication between the business and IT. That has never been easy, but organizations are increasingly recognizing the importance of this kind of cooperation. Additionally, they are now realizing that data management involves more than entering data and running reports. It requires enterprise-wide data management or, more precisely, data governance. They are also becoming keenly aware of the ramifications of poor data quality: dissatisfied customers, confused employees, unhappy stakeholders, and poor bottom-line results.

There was a time—prior to the information explosion—when organizations were easily able to identify any anomalies in their data and adjust accordingly. Data was not considered a corporate asset. It was just one part of running the business, and most executives did not realize—and certainly were not concerned about—data quality.

Today there is a completely different situation. The amount of data each company produces has skyrocketed and shows no signs of decreasing. Coupled with pressures to outperform the competition, comply with a multitude of regulations, and, of course, improve the bottom line, this situation demands that every organization take steps to realize the full value of the data they have. Without data quality and data governance, this cannot be accomplished.

Due to the number of sources, the vast amounts of data and the multiplicity of data types, information quality must be automated. It can no longer be done manually. More importantly, attention to information quality is an ongoing process, and it has to be an integral and continuous part of the entire data governance process.

But let's get back to golf. Playing a good game of golf doesn't just happen. In order to play golf, you need to know the rules of the game. In this book, Tony Fisher outlines the rules of data governance, explaining how to improve data quality and how to plan and implement an effective data governance program.

Two of the key aspects of golf are the course where the game is played and the equipment that is used. Both can either positively or negatively affect the outcome of the game, just as the quality of an organization's data can improve its performance or, if the data quality is poor, result in increased operational costs, poor decisions, and reconciliation problems.

Great golfers appreciate great golf courses. Creating courses that are not only scenic but challenging has been accomplished by notable golf course architects such as A.W. Tillinghast, Donald Ross, and Robert Trent Jones. When playing on a challenging course, the value of a knowledgeable caddy is immeasurable. Filled with the knowledge gleaned from experience, this book is the caddy for your data governance course.

A good golfer also appreciates playing on a course where the greens are well maintained. Putting on a well-maintained green is like putting on carpet because there are no inconsistencies, and the ball runs true. By contrast, putting on greens that are not maintained very well may increase your score (not a good thing in golf) by 6 to 10 strokes. When a corporation does not treat data as an asset (poorly maintained greens), the ball does not run true (inaccurate data produces incorrect and misleading results), and the corporation suffers increased inconsistencies, errors, and even compliance failure.

Golf equipment—drivers, wedges, putters, gloves, shoes—definitely makes a difference in each golfer's game. A stick with a rock tied to the end does not send a drive down the fairway like a Callaway FT-iQ Tour Driver. Other tools used by every self-respecting golfer include subscriptions to several online or print golf periodicals that provide helpful advice on the latest innovations in golf equipment and methodologies for lowering one's handicap. Similarly, to make a difference in their corporations, executives need to become knowledgeable about the methodologies and best practices (the equipment) for data quality and data governance.

As Tony points out in this book, the three major benefits to improving an organization's data are risk mitigation, cost control, and revenue optimization. These benefits are clearly described using real-world examples. This book doesn't present theoretical concepts, but actual problems and solutions from companies you'll surely recognize.

Tony Fisher has definitely scored a hole in one that will benefit all those on the course in their quest for data quality and effective data governance.

Ron Powell
Cofounder and Editorial Director
BeyeNETWORK

Acknowledgments

Author Barbara Grizzuti Harrison said, "There are no original ideas. There are only original people." In writing this book, it has become clear to me just how true these words are. Fortunately for me, and for you as the reader, I have had the privilege of working with and learning from a lot of original people. This book is not necessarily filled with new ideas as much as it is a compilation of ideas—from many people— combined to provide a practical approach to how to improve your business by improving your data. The individuals listed here shared ideas and experiences, and I am indebted to each one of them. Given that there are no original ideas just original people, the most important element becomes who you talk to. I'd like to acknowledge some of the folks who have helped me formulate ideas.

My many colleagues and experts in the data management community have provided a wealth of ideas and inspiration. These friends have been practitioners in helping organizations understand the value that data can bring. They have shared thoughts and information with me and with data professionals around the world. There is a very long list of industry experts, but these select few are ones that, time and time again, provide the rest of us with valuable insight. A special thanks to Jill Dyché and Evan Levy of Baseline Consulting. Few people have the business acumen, technology skills, and just plain common sense that Jill and Evan possess. Special thanks go out to these two good friends for continually providing fresh perspective and improving on the way things are done.

There are many more experts in the field that, both explicitly and implicitly, provided ideas and concepts that have been developed in this book. Fortunately, there are a lot of individuals that provide benefit to the rest of us based on their years of experience, and any attempt to list them will undoubtedly lead to omissions. My apologies to those that provided input that I have not listed here. I did, however, borrow ideas and concepts from Gwen Thomas of The Data Governance Institute, Mike Ferguson of Intelligent Business Strategies, and David Loshin of Knowledge Integrity. I would like to thank these three for the input they have provided me and the input they provide all of us endeavoring to improve our data.

I am thrilled that my good friend Ron Powell was gracious enough to write the foreword for this book. I have known Ron for years, and during that time I have been fortunate to benefit from the many colleagues he has introduced me to. Ron knows so many people that have helped me formulate the concepts in this book, and he has always been instrumental in providing introductions and advice through the years of our relationship.

So, there are no original ideas. There is, however, occasional inspiration. That brings up another of my favorite quotes, this one from Thomas Edison. Edison said, "Genius is one percent inspiration, ninety-nine percent perspiration." That turns out to be true for writing a book as well. Fortunately, the perspiration was a burden shared by a number of my colleagues at DataFlux. I would like to thank all my colleagues at DataFlux for the years of collaboration that have led to the techniques found in this book. Special thanks to Lucia Riley and Daniel Teachey for the continuous suggestions about how to improve the book and make the book more appealing for readers. Scott Batchelor provided a great service in suggesting content and making sure the book was transformed from mere words to the finished product you hold in your hands now. Thanks also to Gail Baker for her outstanding work with our customers to receive permission to showcase their compelling stories in the book.

Catherine L. Traugot provided copious energy into the writing of this book. Her experience and advice from other similar engagements were essential in moving this book from a theoretical exercise to a practical project. Many thanks to her for the months of advice and guidance.

Amongst all of my friends and colleagues at DataFlux, Katie Fabiszak deserves special recognition. Katie is primarily responsible for the idea of writing this book, and she provided considerable input to the content as well as motivation to see the book through to completion. Katie's most beneficial contributions to this book are her knowledge of the subject matter and her uncanny ability to take difficult concepts and break them down into manageable, coherent thoughts.

There is one last group of people to whom I owe special thanks—the biggest thanks go to my family. Although they have yet to fully understand why I would spend time writing a book about data management, I would really like to thank Linda, Andy, and Laura for their patience as I worked long hours on this project. My daughter Laura even asked to read the book (what better endorsement is there?). I hope you get as much enjoyment out of reading this book as I did in writing it.

Introduction

O ver the past couple of decades, I've been a real advocate of encouraging organizations to understand the potential value of their data. At times, it has been frustrating to try to convince organizations that data can be the difference between business success and business failure. More recently, though, the value of data has begun to be better understood and more effectively utilized. If we look back 20 years ago, we were producers of data. For example, we used data for taking and processing orders. And, we produced copious amounts of transaction data. Companies spent a great deal of time inputting data, but very few resources were allocated to doing anything constructive with that data. As a result, the data largely sat unused after a transaction was completed. Data was a necessary part of doing business, but was not being utilized to its full potential.

As technologies and products began to emerge that could facilitate faster data entry, more and more organizations began to view data as a key piece of the business that could be leveraged to improve operations—through sales or cost-reduction or inventory management. But they still lacked the tools to see the data as more than fields in a database. It was as if the data that drove and supported their companies was stored inside a glass case—untouchable and out of reach.

Today, all companies have data. It is an integral part of day-to-day operations. Yet few companies treat data as a strategic asset. It reminds me of the seafaring poem by Samuel Taylor Coleridge:

> Day after day, day after day,
> We stuck, nor breath nor motion;
> As idle as a painted ship
> Upon a painted ocean.

Water, water, everywhere,
And all the boards did shrink;
Water, water, everywhere,
Nor any drop to drink.

—"The Rime of the Ancient Mariner"

While Coleridge most certainly did not have data management in mind when he penned his masterpiece, many companies are in the same boat as the mariner in the poem—stuck in idle day after day, surrounded by data, with no idea how to utilize it to improve their companies.

The pressures on organizations today are ever-increasing: pressures to comply with regulatory and industry standards, pressures to achieve profitability and meet shareholder expectations, pressures to compete in an uncertain and constantly changing economy. To be able to combat these pressures, organizations must rely on consistent, accurate, and reliable data to govern their businesses, regardless of their industries.

In this book, I will use three terms over and over: data quality, data governance, and data management. Data quality examines whether an organization's data is reliable, consistent, up to date, free of duplication, and fit for its purposes. Data governance encompasses the process created to maintain high standards of data quality across the enterprise. Data governance addresses how data enters the organization and who is accountable for it. Using people, process, and technology, your data achieves a quality standard that allows for complete transparency within your organization. Data management refers to a consistent methodology that ensures the deployment of timely and trusted data across the organization.

The demand for data quality and data governance to support critical business initiatives is skyrocketing—and with it the confusion. Executives and shareholders are beginning to realize that data is a strategic asset—and with that, there are mandates issued to ensure that proper data management practices are put in place. Without a sound data strategy and roadmap, even the most experienced executives can lose their way. Organizations often develop business strategies and set directions based on information that is available to executives, but—as I will discuss in this book—that information is often wrong or hopelessly out of date. From the threat of fines for not identifying and reporting terrorist financing to millions of dollars lost because customer data is riddled with errors and duplications, organizations risk not only money but their reputation when they make decisions based on data that cannot be trusted.

IS MY COMPANY READY FOR DATA GOVERNANCE?

Answer these three simple questions to find out if your company is positioned to launch a data governance initiative.

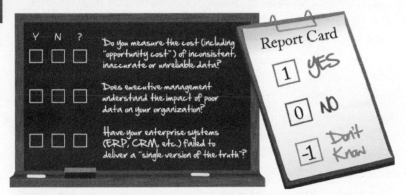

Now, tabulate your score and find the appropriate category below to see if your company is ready for a data governance program.

2–3 points: Your company is ready and prepared. Chances are that you have already seen the impact that good data can have on your organization. You are making important data decisions across the enterprise, but may still need some help achieving all your data goals. To maximize the effectiveness of this book, you may want to focus on the chapters discussing the stages of data governance maturity, to find out where your company falls and to make plans to take the next step.

- Undisciplined (Chapter 6)
- Reactive (Chapter 7)
- Proactive (Chapter 8)
- Governed (Chapter 9)

0–1 points: Even though you may not have all the pieces in place for a data governance program, you can easily identify the areas for improvement. With a few modifications and key personnel additions, you can quickly begin your data governance journey. Chapter 1 will show you how to build the business case for data governance. An effective program involves executive sponsorship, and a strong business case can help achieve this.

Less than zero points: If you fall into this category, don't feel discouraged. As you will read later in this book, the majority of companies are here with you. All it means is that you have some work to do before you have a high level of data governance. But the fact you are reading this book means that you are interested in finding out how your data can become an asset to your company. You have to start somewhere, and following the instructions in this book is a great first step.

Internally, many organizations mistakenly view data, its accuracy, and its collection, as an "IT problem." Past efforts to solve "IT problems" have often engulfed the organization in expensive, multiyear projects that have not seemed to pay the dividends promised, and the projects have frequently failed. Executives know they want trusted data; they just don't know how to effectively reach that point. When they have been burned by approving expensive IT projects that never delivered the intended results and promised return on investment (ROI), executives can be reluctant to invest in additional programs.

In this book I will outline how to get your data to work for you without breaking the bank or scrapping your current solutions. I will first discuss the business case for ridding your organization of unreliable data and the opportunities that exist when you treat data as a strategic asset. Regardless of the industry that your company is in or the business issues that you face, I will tell you how managing your data is strategic to your goals.

Next I will build the case for creating a data quality and data governance framework. This framework will allow you to improve your data in incremental steps. This is important because too many organizations have been sold an application with a "this will solve all your problems" pitch. But your business is not static. New applications will emerge; existing ones will be improved; and old, legacy applications will be retired. All of these applications and solutions need to be viewed through the lens of trusted data. This book will help organizations determine their capacity for data governance by measuring their data maturity, and it will provide a methodical step-by-step program for successful data quality and data governance initiatives.

As I have worked with different organizations over the years, I have concluded that every company falls into one of four maturity stages, based on their IT and business practices. Organizations are either undisciplined, reactive, proactive, or governed with respect to the way they manage their data. I will provide an in-depth look at the technology adoption and business capabilities that are required at each stage to move an organization to the next stage. In the final part, I will lay out a methodology that encompasses the involvement of both business and IT professionals for collaborating on the establishment of data standards as well as the processes and technologies required for successful data quality and data governance.

Along the way, I will use real-world examples to illustrate how actual companies are using data quality and data governance strategies to better their businesses (an icon will be placed in the margins so that you can easily identify where these examples are). I have been fortunate to work with some amazing companies over the years. Undoubtedly, you are in a similar situation to many of them. They are good, solid companies, but have not been able to keep up with the vast amounts of data that reside within their organizations. Often, a small change in the way they approach data makes a significant difference in their ability to optimize revenue, manage costs, and mitigate risk.

Data is not "IT's problem." It is every employee's problem. It is every executive's problem. And seeking a way to constructively and economically address data issues is paramount to the success of your organization.

There are two mantras I repeat time and time again throughout this book. These are important truths to remember as you embark on your journey to data governance. First, data quality and data governance should *never* be considered a one-time project. A quality culture must be established, and it is an ongoing, continuous process. Second, no organization can tackle enterprise-wide data quality and data governance all at once. To be successful, your journey must be an evolutionary one. Start small and take achievable steps that can be measured along the way.

PART ONE

Building the Business Case
for Data Governance

CHAPTER 1

Making the Case for Better Data

The whole is more than the sum of its parts.

—ARISTOTLE (384–322 B.C.), PHILOSOPHER

EXECUTIVE OVERVIEW

One of the biggest mistakes that organizations make is to approach data as a technology asset. It is not. It is a corporate asset and needs to be treated and funded as a corporate asset. Justification for data management projects lies in the ability to create a business plan based on the benefit to an organization. Executives want to know how a data

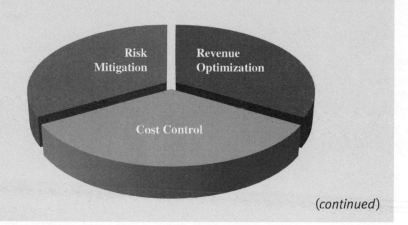

(continued)

(*Continued*)

management initiative will enhance the business. To do this, any attempt to improve your organization must emphasize these benefits:

- Risk mitigation
- Revenue optimization
- Cost control

Building the business case is the first and most important step.

REMEMBER

1. Data quality and data governance should *never* be considered a one-time project. A quality culture must be established as an ongoing, continuous process.

2. No organization can tackle enterprisewide data quality and data governance all at once. To be successful, your journey must be evolutionary. Start small and take achievable steps that can be measured along the way.

Many organizations find that they cannot rely on the information that serves as the very foundation of their business. Unreliable data—whether about customers, products, or suppliers—hinders understanding and hurts the bottom line. It seems a rather simple concept: Better data leads to better decisions, which ultimately leads to better business. So why don't executives take data quality and data governance more seriously? In my experience, this lack of attention to data severely and negatively impacts numerous organizations—some of which will be highlighted in this book. We all need to understand that we are seeing a shift in the way that we think about and treat data. Successful organizations are moving from a focus on *producing data* to a focus on *consuming data*.

For most organizations, this journey is just beginning. And for most organizations, this journey begins with education. Part of my reason for writing this book is to help organizations establish a solid data foundation as they embark on this journey.

This is what happens in organizations today. Data is typically somebody else's problem—until something bad happens. The CEO of a plumbing manufacturer learned this the hard way a few years ago. One of his major manufacturing plants burned to the ground, and the CEO was eager to immediately inform customers of the situation. He asked for a list of products that were expected to be manufactured in the destroyed plant and for a list of customers that were expecting delivery.

This CEO, like any chief executive, undoubtedly believed that this information was a readily available corporate asset. In the era of business applications like enterprise resource planning (ERP), customer relationship management (CRM), and data warehouses, it should have been a simple request. It wasn't. The finance department provided a list of everybody who had bought something, but that department didn't know the product delivery schedule. The sales office knew who every customer was and what they had purchased, but not where the products would be manufactured. The manufacturing plant had a delivery list of what to produce, but not a full inventory of what was in the production pipeline.

Of course, the closest thing to what the CEO needed—the delivery list—was destroyed in the fire. Eventually, the IT department cobbled together an incomplete list and presented this to the CEO. Predictably, the CEO became frustrated ("How can you *not* know who our customers are?"). In the end, the CEO decided data wasn't such a dull topic at all. It was integral to his business.

The CEO—and this entire organization—realized Aristotle's message. The sum of the data in the individual systems did not accurately depict the whole of the business. Aristotle was one of the greatest of the ancient Greek philosophers and is still considered one of the most visionary thinkers of all time. As a pioneer in the field of study of metaphysics, Aristotle sought to develop a way of reasoning by which it would be possible to learn as much as possible about an entity.

While most discussions about data do not start with philosophical references, it is important to note that the crux of Aristotle's philosophy is applicable to most enterprises. Exhaustive efforts at studying, cataloging, and accessing information led Aristotle to the observation that the whole is more than the sum of its parts. Like Aristotle's quest to know and understand, data management is about learning everything there is to know about your organization—and more specifically, learning everything there is to know about the data that is required to run your organization.

The quality, accessibility, and usability of data have an impact on every organization, but the issue rarely captures the attention of executives. Mergers and acquisitions, creative marketing campaigns, and outsourcing are much hotter topics that can create the sales spikes or cost cutting that shareholders like to see.

Yet most of these high-profile initiatives fail or underperform if the data cannot be trusted. That creative marketing campaign may cost too much per sale if the customer list is riddled with redundant or inaccurate customer records. Buying another company to gain new customers is an expensive mistake if the purchased company turns out to share the same customer base. The cost savings of outsourcing are erased if the business cannot gather and measure customer complaints that emerge if the outsourced help desk isn't doing its job. Inconsistent, inaccurate, and unreliable data has a huge impact on organizations. According to Gartner, a leading technology firm, "Through 2011, 75 percent of organizations will experience significantly reduced revenue growth potential and increased costs due to the failure to introduce data quality assurance and coordinate it with their data integration and metadata management strategies (0.7 probability)."[1]

High-quality, trusted data serves another purpose—one that executives wish they didn't have to address. It keeps them out of trouble. Any financial services company must report potentially laundered money to a regulatory agency to avoid fines—or even jail time. An oil company needs to know which state-owned pipelines it uses to stay current with local regulations. Across the compliance arena, quality data can make the difference between spending money on fines or investing in the business.

New compliance regulations have illuminated a pressing need that has always been a critical part of running a successful business. Twenty-five years ago, it was common for a publicly-traded company to remain in the dark about profits and revenue until days before the quarter ended. Financial planning has now grown sophisticated enough that CEOs of publicly-traded companies are expected to project revenue and income and alert shareholders if the company is falling short. The quality of the data is critical—and more than one CEO has been shown the door when the company failed to get it right.

Even with the millions and billions of dollars invested in sophisticated information management systems and applications, CEOs are still getting hopelessly burned by incomplete, poorly managed, and inaccessible data. In early 2008, the French bank Société Générale (SG) took $7 billion in losses after a rogue trader made unauthorized trades for many months—this loss represented almost all the profits SG had made in the past few years. The trader apparently covered his tracks by manipulating the way the company's computer systems worked, but better data control and consistent monitoring would have uncovered the illegal trades—well before $7 billion evaporated.

Having money launderers as customers, overpaying for pipeline rights, rogue derivatives trading—these all seem to have very little in common. But there is one major commonality: These types of risk can all be minimized with better management of data.

Dwelling on the negatives is easy when it comes to data because disasters in data quality make the headlines. I have been on the phone with enough panicked executives to collect scare stories that could keep a CEO from ever sleeping again. But there is another side to data quality—how properly managed information turns to gold and creates the aha! moment that drives productivity and innovation. It does not always come with a precise return on investment (ROI)—since companies so often do not have a benchmark for how much errant data is costing them. The value of good data comes instead with what one business executive described as "leveraging maximum value from our investments."

BUILDING THE BUSINESS CASE

In business today, it is impossible to get executive sponsorship or funding for any initiative without a clear and compelling business justification. How is spending this money going to help us increase revenue? How can this program improve the business? Can we afford to fund this initiative at this time? To make an investment in your data—and to ensure that it becomes a strategic corporate asset—you must first build the business case. The reason to better manage data is to improve your business. When it comes to building the business case, you have to document the potential benefits for your organization. As I have already indicated, there are three major benefits to improving your company's data that are front-of-mind with executives in every organization: risk mitigation, cost control, and revenue optimization.

Risk mitigation is the most likely reason a company focuses on data quality, according to an *Information Age* survey of 279 companies.[2]

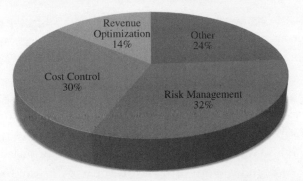

FIGURE 1.1   **Why do companies focus on data quality?**

Almost one-third of companies said risk management (which encompasses compliance and regulatory issues) was a key driver of data quality (see Figure 1.1).

A few years ago, I worked with a company that had just completed a  difficult and time-consuming acquisition. On the surface, the acquisition looked great. The two companies had some complementary products, but there was a fair amount of competitive products. The idea was to streamline the product offerings and reduce costs by combining redundant functions. Since the company that was acquired generated 60 percent as much revenue as the acquiring company, the merger would create a company with substantially more income. In reality, though, the results were not so satisfactory.

The reason for this underperformance was a lack of knowledge about the new company. One of the things the new parent company never discovered during the due diligence process was that almost half of the acquired company's customers were already customers of the acquiring company. The amount of revenue that the merged company generated was substantially less than anticipated. This was a huge risk that could have been mitigated with better data management. By understanding who the customers really were, the new parent company would have been able to identify the scores of duplicate customers and would have had that information at the ready during the due diligence process.

According to 30 percent of the respondents in the *Information Age* survey, cost control is the second-most-likely reason companies look at data quality or data governance,. Properly managed data can help companies unearth numerous areas where money is leaking out of the organization. And, with a diligent data quality approach, you can deliver significant gains for your organization.

 A global chemical manufacturer wanted to control costs when it purchased items. More than 600 people worldwide had purchasing authority, and they were inconsistent in the way they coded items at the time of purchase. These item codes were intended to provide a way to aggregate and sort products purchased, providing a better view of the organization's spending habits. Unfortunately, the inconsistent product code entries did little to help with spend analysis. The company didn't know what it was buying, nor did it have an understanding of what it was buying from its different suppliers. This prevented it from attaining any sort of bulk purchasing discounts. By incorporating product data rules, automating the classification, analyzing the results, and making changes to its purchasing process, the company now estimates that it will save up to 5 percent on its annual indirect spend of $3 billion. That's a number that would excite any executive.

The third reason—and one I think companies have yet to address sufficiently—is revenue optimization. Only 14 percent of respondents in the *Information Age* survey ranked revenue optimization as the reason to improve data quality. Using information wisely to become more agile and responsive is so simple that it is amazing how many companies dismiss it. If done properly, data management can pay for itself in a short time.

Risk Mitigation: One Version of the Truth Helps Retail Bankers Manage Risk

Many retail banks have product-oriented risk management systems (for instance, a risk management system for loans, another for credit cards, another for banking [savings and accounts], and another for mortgages). There is often no single integrated customer-oriented risk management system to see the true risk exposure of every customer level for all credit-risk products that a customer holds. If a customer fails to make a loan payment, the bank can often take up to several weeks to change the credit limits on credit cards held by the same customer. Because there is no single integrated operational view of customer and product data, the bank risks an increase in bad debt.

However, with a single view of a customer, shown in Figure 1.2, banks can easily view the total exposure with each customer, since

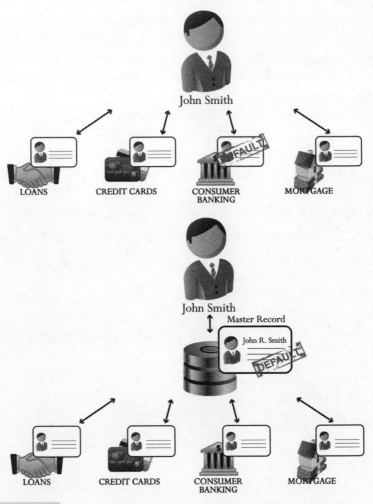

FIGURE 1.2   **A single, rationalized view of the customer can result in improved risk management**

they can be made aware of all transactions and how the transactions are related.

Cost Control: Manufacturing Costs Rise When Data Isn't Integrated

Manufacturing operations are highly dependent on shared information. The customer data created in sales is needed in customer service, marketing, finance, and distribution. Product development data is needed in manufacturing, planning, and stores. Order data is needed throughout the enterprise. Maintaining consistency and preventing conflicts to this data across operational applications and processes is critical to business operations. If product development wants to package a product in 16 oz. bottles, instead of 8 oz. cans (Figure 1.3), manufacturing needs to reset its equipment, buyers need to purchase bottles and make sure they are delivered to the plants, and stocking specialists need to work with retailers to display the new size. Basic errors in the data chain can lead to manufacturing errors, additional distribution costs to make up for shortages caused by those errors, oversupply in distribution centers, and customer dissatisfaction.

FIGURE 1.3   Shifting manufacturing to produce 16 oz. bottles can be disastrous unless data issues are resolved

REVENUE OPTIMIZATION: HOW A LEADING RETAILER REVOLUTIONIZED INVENTORY MANAGEMENT THROUGH DATA MANAGEMENT

Wal-Mart may be one of the best in the world at revenue optimization based on consumer demand. Wal-Mart's supply chain technologies allow it to replenish inventory on the shelf in less than three days—not just from the warehouse to the shelf, but from the manufacturer to the shelf. While other retailers struggle with getting adequate product on their shelves, Wal-Mart has reached back to the assembly line itself to streamline their supply chain programs. That's why Wal-Mart shoppers are almost always able to find the right item when they need it.

The key to Wal-Mart's success is in the quality and management of their supply chain data. Within 14 seconds of the purchase of a product at Wal-Mart, the Wal-Mart central warehouse is notified of the change in inventory. In addition, manufacturers of the product are made aware of the sale so that as inventory moves from the warehouse to the store, the products in the warehouse will be replenished by the manufacturer. Even the raw material suppliers that the manufacturer needs are alerted, so that they can supply the manufacturer the necessary raw materials. And this process is repeated throughout the supply chain.

Can every company replicate the Wal-Mart model? A 14-second inventory change notification might be difficult without other processes in place. But with high-quality data flowing throughout your systems, you can more accurately model your supply chain to react to market changes, customer requests, and supplier dynamics.

In today's competitive environment, with high customer expectations, employee satisfaction, and regulatory demands—it is essential to run your business as efficiently as possible. The key to better business is better data, managing and funding your data infrastructure as you would your other corporate assets. This is achievable only if you build data management and data governance processes based on business requirements. To do this, concentrate on risk mitigation, cost control, and revenue optimization as you build your business justification for better data.

INTEGRATED, QUALITY DATA MEANS BETTER BUSINESS

Suppose that you are thinking to yourself, *Yes, I have already been sold a bill of goods for an enterprise-wide solution that would mitigate my risk, control my expenses or optimize my revenue, and if you want to advocate for another type of enterprise-wide solution, I'm going to toss this book in the recycling bin.* Well, stop! No one wants you to scrap your existing investments. What businesses need is an integration strategy built on a firm foundation of quality data across applications. This will not replace, but rather leverage existing strategic enterprise-wide investments, and even help the one-off solutions work better across the enterprise.

If you use a handheld device like a BlackBerry, you are pretty familiar with the idea of synchronization. You do it daily to make sure your e-mail and calendar info syncs up. Companies need to do the same thing with their enterprise-wide and non-enterprise-wide data to create consistent and trusted data. Without data quality and data integration in an enterprise environment, business processes will still be plagued by defects caused by inability to eradicate data errors, and an inability to integrate, consolidate, share and synchronize core operational data, master data and historical analytical data across the enterprise.

Even if you aren't using an enterprise-wide application, data quality and data integration issues can bedevil companies. Uncontrolled and unmanaged data regularly wreak havoc on business operations, decision making, performance management, and compliance. Business operations are affected because employees, customers, partners, and suppliers struggle to find information. Also, incomplete and inaccurate data can cause operational process errors and inefficiencies, as well as the inability to respond quickly to business changes.

To the BlackBerry user, the synchronization process is automatic, fast, and easy—just push a button and—*voilà!* Business executives often wonder why automating one of their processes doesn't end up saving money. For starters, it is not uncommon to see companies rekeying data across multiple applications as part of an operational process. Keying anything into any system involves humans who are prone to making mistakes. Synchronization is also often considerably more complex than it needs to be, because subsets of data are maintained in multiple systems (often with partial duplication) without creating one single integrated view. All of this can result in increased operational costs and customer dissatisfaction that, in turn, can impact profitability and growth.

Poor data quality—and the lack of data integration for single integrated views of application data—can lead to unsatisfactory decisions. If multiple data warehouses across the enterprise are fractured with conflicting subsets of data, the problem can lead directly to performance management problems. One example is a company whose employees respond to data that can't be reconciled by creating their own personal spreadsheets. Then, they attach their spreadsheets to a distribution e-mail. Soon, the company is awash in spreadsheets that don't match up. After a while, the owners of the different spreadsheets begin to realize that something isn't quite right, although it still feels right. The assumption is that the data is correct—when it is often invalid and out of date. This leads to decision making that is flawed. Even when the actual truth from the dispersed spreadsheets is discovered, the results are delayed decisions and untimely responses. And if causing internal trouble isn't enough, the lack of integrated data and poor data quality can also affect a company's ability to remain compliant amid growing regulatory burdens. Regulation violations can bring expensive prosecutions and penalties as well as loss of shareholder value, customer confidence, and corporate reputation. Even when a company sets very high compliance standards, violations due to defective data may make it impossible to meet those standards.

INFORMATION FOR EVERY MEMBER OF THE EXECUTIVE TEAM

As much data as flows through businesses today, executives often tell me they do not know where to begin to get the information they need. In some companies, the IT department is keeper of data, and a simple question such as "How many units did we sell of this product vs. a similar product packaged differently?" can involve a request to IT that will take a week or more to turn around. Lengthy delays fuel the pessimistic mindset rampant in many companies where data is viewed as sensitive and in need of safeguarding.

In still other companies, each C-level executive has built her own silo of information. The chief marketing officer (CMO) has data on sales and marketing efforts and may be able to create automated marketing campaigns. The chief financial officer (CFO) is tracking dollars and cents, using a solution unique to the world of finance. The executive vice president of merchandising or manufacturing sets up his own supply chain, buying and planning systems.

There are, of course, problems with each of these approaches. When IT holds the data captive, executives tend to request the same type of static report over and over, because asking for unique reports is often a time-consuming exercise in futility. Figure 1.4 illustrates that when information is managed in silos, there is no single version of the truth. The CMO may be raving about a marketing campaign bumping sales over last year, while the CFO stares at a sheet with data that suggests the exact opposite.

Each executive may manage very different worlds, but they need to work from the same data foundation—and they can benefit from exposure to the kind of data that other executives use and manage. For instance, the CMO is typically responsible for retention, market share, branding, cross-sell opportunities, and up-sell effectiveness. How many CMOs, though, can readily determine whether a new marketing campaign for a lower-margin product or service is actually cannibalizing existing high-margin customers? Meanwhile, the executive vice president of manufacturing's finely honed supply chain may not be flexible enough for the CMO's plan to market products in several different types and sizes of packaging.

The CFO is looking at the business from a completely different perspective, because she is responsible for the financial performance across the organization. In publicly-held companies, the CFO needs to forecast reliable earnings expectations. In both private and public companies, the CFO is constantly under pressure to maximize performance and value, establish key performance indicators (KPIs), predict trends, and align strategic goals. The CFO also shares some of the burden of regulatory compliance. A CFO isn't responsible for a supply chain disruption, but without that information the forecasts can't be reported accurately.

In advanced organizations, the chief information officer (CIO) is more business focused, understanding the needs of the other executives, helping align IT and business, and explaining the value of reaching one version of the truth. This person provides a critical role in establishing the data sharing that is needed to make the business run better. This is not an easy task—even starting may be difficult. The vast majority of companies have

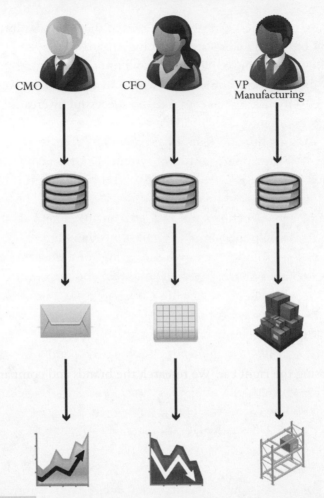

FIGURE 1.4   How can siloed information affect the business? if the cmo views a marketing campaign as a success based on the number of orders taken, but those orders are for losses, the CFO will have a different view of the outcome. and if the manufacturing team isn't clued in on all the products sold, customers may find the shelves empty with a long lead time before restocking is possible.

multiple applications and systems, and executives are quite fond of their own solutions. Business users, meanwhile, maintain—or clamor for—a solution that solves their specific problem. Championing an enterprise-wide approach involves a huge upfront cost, a great deal of risk, and the potential dissatisfaction of business users who are tied to their siloed solutions. Realistically, the CIO can't advocate scrapping a myriad of systems, solutions, and software that are in use. The CIO can't impose a one-size-fits-all solution, even if such a solution were available in the market today. But the CIO *can* focus on making the organization successful by creating a collaborative, aligned, and integrated data environment.

Adding data quality and data governance to the existing data silos or the enterprise-wide applications and systems can fix many of the problems a CIO faces in data management, while limiting the pain to the business users.

Even though the benefits of successful data management can be substantial, getting to that point shouldn't consume you. Improvement is not about buying one solution, scrapping existing solutions, or patching together 20 disparate systems. The process is not about the next 12 months being the "Year We Get Our Data in Order." This is a process that is best done by taking one step at a time, one project at a time, one action at a time—while always focusing on the business reasons.

I like cars, so I like car analogies. We tend to spend a lot of time and effort choosing the right car. We research the brands and comparison shop, and when it's all finished and we drive off the lot, we think "Phew, glad that's over with." Achieving quality data is not like the process of buying the car. But it is like the process of maintaining the car. It is putting the right gas in, getting the oil checked, replacing worn tires. It is the routine, everyday things that are critical when it comes to keeping the car running and maintaining its value. Quality data keeps your business running smoothly, it keeps your company's value high, and ultimately it keeps your company in business. Period.

■ NOTES

1. Donald Feinberg. "Poor-Quality Data: The Sure Way to Lose Business and Attract Auditors," 2006.
2. "Data Governance: Protecting and Exploiting a Key Business Asset," *Information Age* Research Report, Michelle Price, February 22, 2008.

CHAPTER 2

Risk Mitigation: How Quality Data Keeps Your Company Out of Trouble

A danger foreseen is half avoided.

—Proverb

Executive Overview

Will you be in business next week? Next year? In 20 years? Without sound risk assessment and mitigation, you won't. By definition, risk assessment and avoidance require the collection of data from around your organization. Risk areas of critical importance include:

- Corporate governance
- Mergers and acquisitions
- Corporate reputation
- Compliance
- Fraud detection
- Risk assessment

This chapter explores the connection between corporate risk and corporate data.

(continued)

(Continued)

REMEMBER

1. Data quality and data governance should *never* be considered a one-time project. A quality culture must be established as an ongoing, continuous process.

2. No organization can tackle enterprise-wide data quality and data governance all at once. To be successful, your journey must be evolutionary. Start small and take achievable steps that can be measured along the way.

Most executives become successful not by avoiding risk, but by understanding and embracing it. Business magazines tout executives who take risky gambles on far-flung ventures that pay off handsomely. What executive has not wanted to be described as "daring" or "adventurous"— all words closely aligned with "risk taker"?

However, executives know that not all risk is created equal. There is calculated risk—done with the full knowledge of the possible consequences. Unfortunately, there is also the type of risk that is believed to be calculated until it turns out the calculation was predicated on less than optimal information. This risk is unnecessary risk; I call it misguided risk. And then there is the risk that hides in companies in the form of unethical employees and sloppy business practices—negative risk. Executives spend a great deal of time studying risk, figuring out how to avoid the negative versions and embrace the calculated varieties. But they often fail to understand just how poor data quality magnifies the negative risk and makes calculated risk difficult to achieve.

> There are three types of risk:
> 1. Calculated
> 2. Misguided
> 3. Negative

Risk analysis and assessment come in many forms. Regardless of the risk area, the bottom line is that managing and mitigating risk helps ensure that the company will be in business tomorrow, next week, and next year. To mitigate risks, executives often put too much emphasis on the people involved and not enough on the information that underpins the decisions. Is mitigating risk about hiring the right risk compliance officer? Or is it about training supervisors to watch for risky behavior? The best risk takers are the smartest people in the company, right? Not necessarily. People are important, but it is the information companies have on customers, products, and finances that is at the core of any risk mitigation effort. The best risk taker is an informed risk taker. Naturally, high-quality data can mitigate risks associated with regulatory compliance, fraud, corporate sustainability, corporate reputation, mergers and acquisitions, corporate governance, and many other areas that are critical to the future success of any business. All of these risk areas will be better managed by understanding and rationalizing data from across the entire organization.

Nonetheless, we want to believe that risky behavior that results in fines, losses, and public scorn is tied to the behavior of one person or a group of people—an ethically compromised accountant or a compliance department asleep at the wheel, for example. A focus on people, their poor work habits or pure fraudulent behavior provides a clear villain. It is interesting to read about Société Générale's "rogue trader" and the company's co-chief executive describing him as "mentally weak" with potential insiders helping him. But it may not be so compelling to wonder what automated, data-driven, process could have been in place to catch him. One newspaper article about Société Générale featured a sidebar describing a "Who's Who" of rogue traders from around the globe who have cost their firms anywhere from $550 million to $6.6 billion in losses.[1] People like Nicholas Leeson, the young trader whose unauthorized trades in derivatives lost $1.3 billion and brought down England's oldest merchant bank, Barings, in 1995. And Yasuo Hamanaka, a copper trader who cost Sumitomo Corporation $2.6 billion.

There will always be individuals with a less-than-ethical approach to business. But how do we monitor and detect these individuals as well as calculate the risk associated with day-to-day business? We are inclined, after all, to see this situation much like a Hollywood movie with some tireless fraud investigator sleuthing out a corrupt bad guy. Indeed, the red flags embedded in the internal controls at Société Générale did play a role in bringing down the trader. Sadly, for the bank, the flags just did not fly often enough. Also, take into account the serious problems that faced financial institutions that were unable to judge the quality of mortgages sold in the secondary market. It is obvious that risk mitigation at some of the most sophisticated institutions in the world is just not working as it should.

True risk mitigation is tied to the quality of the data coupled with a set of internal controls, or business rules, that quickly and simply flag issues. Sifting through all the data rapidly is paramount to success. One of the details emerging from the Société Générale story is that the reports that would have revealed the trader's actions did not get produced frequently enough. They only were generated in an effort to meet regulatory compliance. The data was all there; it just wasn't being used. Meanwhile, the control systems that were in place and were designed for day-to-day use were ineffective and were easily thwarted. It is the combination of data quality and robust internal controls and processes that will ultimately reduce risk in an organization.

Managing and Mitigating Risk Effectively

As companies grow and acquire new businesses, the potential for risk multiplies. For every rogue trade, there are numerous examples involving companies with small data errors causing big problems. And even though these errors may not make the front page, they can have a tremendous impact on a company's ability to stay competitive.

A global oil and gas company provides a good example of how seemingly  inconsequential errors can potentially cause big problems. Oil moves through pipes that are owned by different entities. In the United States, in many instances, states own the pipelines and charge different access fees to companies pumping oil through those pipelines. This global company used data quality technology to detect inaccuracies in their pipeline access fees.

In one example, the information for Arkansas was coded as "AK" instead of "AR," and payments were sent to Alaska instead of Arkansas. This proved to be a double risk as fines for nonpayment would be levied from Arkansas while payment was going to Alaska for pipeline access that wasn't used. In an initial test with data quality software, finding and fixing this one problem encouraged the company to roll out a data quality initiative throughout the entire organization.

The passage of the USA PATRIOT Act, OFAC (Office of Foreign Assets Control), airline no-fly lists, and similar legislation overseas, have caused companies to see the liability in seemingly innocuous errors. These "watch list compliance" rules require financial institutions to report, within 30 days, anyone on the government's list of terrorist, narcotic criminal, money laundering, or other specifically designated individuals who transact business with that institution. Within 10 days of a watch list compliance implementation with a large, multinational bank, it was discovered that its internal systems had previously missed the identification of two individuals on the watch list. That might not seem like much, unless you know that one unintentionally unreported transaction can net you a $1 million fine. An intentionally unreported transaction can result in a *$10 million fine and a prison term*. The price of high-quality data is much less than the two potential fines. That does not even factor in the "intangible" penalties, including the loss of credibility and investor confidence.

However, it is not just banks and brokerages that must pay attention to this example. According to the PATRIOT Act, the term "financial institution" includes the companies we typically think of as providing financial services, as well as currency exchanges, precious metals dealers, travel agencies, telegraph companies, casinos, real estate agencies, car or boat dealers, and the U.S. Postal Service. This means these types of companies must report transactions to be compliant with the law.

Complicating the requirements is the fact that few organizations have a central store of accurate customer data. Data could be stored in operational systems, databases, applications or within individual business units. Pulling the data together to begin matching customers can be problematic. Matching technology, as shown in Figure 2.1, which intelligently identifies relationships between different data entities, can help in any data quality initiative.

Matching customers to watch lists is not as simple as a one-to-one matching activity. There are too many John Smiths in the world to simply look for that name on the watch list and match it to a customer database. Instead, institutions must include other identifying information (birth date, social security number, country of origin). And even then, the different naming conventions of different countries can trip up the matching process. What might appear to be a first name in one country could be a

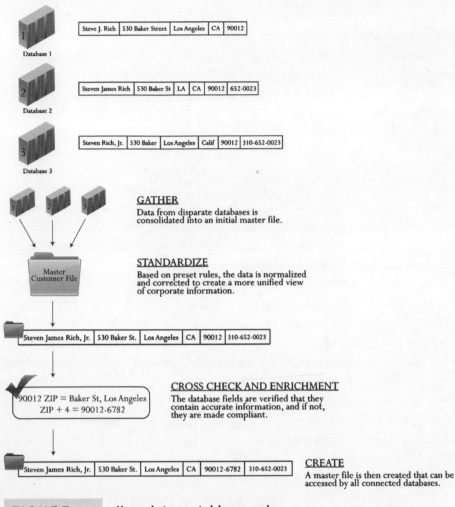

| Steve J. Rich | 530 Baker Street | Los Angeles | CA | 90012 |

Database 1

| Steven James Rich | 530 Baker St | LA | CA | 90012 | 652-0023 |

Database 2

| Steven Rich, Jr. | 530 Baker | Los Angeles | Calif | 90012 | 310-652-0023 |

Database 3

GATHER
Data from disparate databases is consolidated into an initial master file.

Master Customer File

STANDARDIZE
Based on preset rules, the data is normalized and corrected to create a more unified view of corporate information.

| Steven James Rich, Jr. | 530 Baker St. | Los Angeles | CA | 90012 | 310-652-0023 |

90012 ZIP = Baker St, Los Angeles
ZIP + 4 = 90012-6782

CROSS CHECK AND ENRICHMENT
The database fields are verified that they contain accurate information, and if not, they are made compliant.

| Steven James Rich, Jr. | 530 Baker St. | Los Angeles | CA | 90012-6782 | 310-652-0023 |

CREATE
A master file is then created that can be accessed by all connected databases.

FIGURE 2.1   How data matching works

surname or title in another country. Address formats also vary; postal codes and street numbers appear in different locations in various countries. And anyone with a criminal background would likely use an alias—which can further complicate matching results.

Another large, multinational financial institution had an installed system used by compliance officers to flag suspicious client activities. The system sent the compliance team a high number of "false positives"—transactions that looked suspicious but were actually valid—to review and verify

each day. Through matching technology, the institution was able to customize match rules as conditions changed. The company immediately saw a reduction in false positives and increased the accuracy of matches between transactional data and third-party lists. Most important, compliance officers are not wasting their time chasing after false positives but can, instead, focus on transactions much more likely to be suspect.

ACHIEVING TRANSPARENCY WITH STRONG DATA GOVERNANCE

Other regulations are not dependent on watch lists, but do require consistent and accurate data. Take the example of Sarbanes-Oxley (SOX) legislation and the corporate meltdown that birthed it: Enron. The Houston-based energy company was one of the world's largest in 2000, with $111 billion in revenue. *Fortune* magazine named it "Most Innovative Company" for several years running. Unfortunately, the magazine writers did not know about the company's creative, off-the-books accounting that successfully hid millions in losses before the house of cards executives built came tumbling down.

SOX was created to counter practices like Enron's by requiring greater transparency in accounting and financial disclosure. It raised the level of responsibility and accountability. Instead of just facing shareholder wrath and a drop in stock price, a publicly-held company's executives now face criminal penalties. The accounting and financial transparency that are now required means companies have to operate with the best possible data.

Take into consideration the case of a large loan organization that purchases, securitizes, and invests in the secondary mortgage market. The company had already received some negative publicity for reporting inaccurate financial information, and with the passage of SOX, it knew it needed to get its data in order. In the past, each business unit was responsible for data quality and the creation of its own data quality rules. The process was slow and changes to rules took weeks or months to implement. Through data investigation and discovery techniques, the company was able to correct erroneous or duplicate records. A consistent set of business rules was then created that worked across business units on key metrics like loan-to-value ratios and unpaid balances. By ensuring that its federally-mandated reporting was built on high-quality, consistent data, the company is now much more confident about its quarterly and annual financial reports.

BEYOND GOVERNMENT COMPLIANCE: PROACTIVELY AVOIDING RISK

Risk mitigation is not just about keeping clear of the long arm of the law. As companies that traded in subprime mortgages have discovered—you don't have to be facing government fines to still find yourself publicly embarrassed and in a great deal of financial trouble. The subprime mortgage fiasco is a good example of a way that businesses could have proactively used data quality to reduce risk.

Let's think back to how you acquired a home mortgage 20 years ago. You met with a banker or broker in person toting a thick file folder of "proof" that you were a good risk: W-2 statements, paycheck stubs, bank statements, and a detailed list of previous addresses. During the credit checks, the broker might even call your HR department to double-check on your employment status and salary history.

Fast forward to two years ago. Customers acquired a mortgage online with nothing more than a quick credit check. In some cases, subprime lenders barely bothered to double-check any of the information gathered. Housing prices were rising, after all, and the mortgages were bundled and sold as fast as they were issued. The loan originator had washed its hands of any risk long before the homeowner missed the first payment.

However, there were some checks in place, meant to assess risk. For example, loan packages were "rated" using some of the same criteria from the days of the thick file folder. But as an article in the *New York Times* reported,[2] the rating agency typically had 24 hours or less to rate a package and did so with the skimpiest of details. Likewise, mortgage package buyers or those creating mortgage-backed securities, knew very little about the underlying risk associated with the mortgages. Even though the checks were in place, without the appropriate data they were virtually useless. With sound data management in place, the problems could have been avoided.

FIGHTING FRAUD WITH ACCURATE DATA

Accurate and trusted data is a fraudster's worst nightmare. Unlike paper

files that sit in desks, matching processes can be run on well-managed data to unearth all sorts of fraudulent behavior. A classic example is the Medicaid/Medicare provider who uses data matching and resolution technology to find patients or physicians who submit a claim multiple times— with just a little change—hoping the claims will not attract attention and, instead, be paid multiple times. This solution employs time-tested, sophisticated matching technology that flags similar claims and alerts company officials to the possibility of fraud.

Figure 2.2 provides another example of how matching technology can mitigate fraud risk, this time involving a client in the wireless telecommunications sector. The company paid independent agents to resell mobile phone service. The agents got a larger commission for adding a new customer than they did for resigning an existing customer. Some of the agents thought they would take advantage of the system by resigning an existing customer under a slightly different name. For example, existing mobile phone customer Robert R. Jones was now "new customer" Bob Jones. By using matching and identity management technology and by enriching the process with additional data —like address and phone number—the mobile phone provider was quickly able to eliminate this fraud and reduce its commission outlay by millions of dollars per year.

REDUCING THE RISK IN MERGERS AND ACQUISITIONS

Most of us could rattle off the names of mergers and acquisitions that flopped. The promised uptick in revenues and profits did not occur, the increase in market share never materialized, and the efficiencies that were supposed to be gleaned failed to happen.

While it is easy to blame a lawyer, accountant, consultant, or strategist for failing to see the weak spots in a merger or acquisition, often the real fault lies within the data. Poorly managed data can keep mergers and acquisitions from achieving their promise.

One of the main reasons to acquire or merge with a company is to expand the customer base. But this may not be as obvious as it seems on the surface.

WITHOUT MATCHING

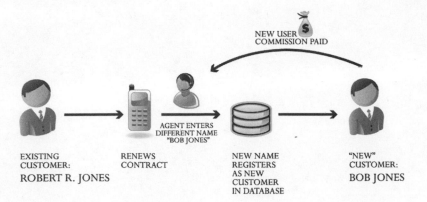

NEW USER
COMMISSION PAID

AGENT ENTERS
DIFFERENT NAME
"BOB JONES"

EXISTING
CUSTOMER:
ROBERT R. JONES

RENEWS
CONTRACT

NEW NAME
REGISTERS
AS NEW
CUSTOMER
IN DATABASE

"NEW"
CUSTOMER:
BOB JONES

WITH MATCHING

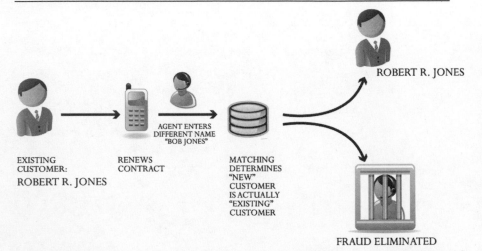

ROBERT R. JONES

AGENT ENTERS
DIFFERENT NAME
"BOB JONES"

EXISTING
CUSTOMER:
ROBERT R. JONES

RENEWS
CONTRACT

MATCHING
DETERMINES
"NEW"
CUSTOMER
IS ACTUALLY
"EXISTING"
CUSTOMER

FRAUD ELIMINATED

FIGURE 2.2   **(a) Without Matching: Mobile phone sales agents were entering existing customers as new customers by using a slightly different name. The result was a higher commission being paid to the agent.**

(b) With Matching: After deploying matching technology, the company was able to detect the fraud by reconciling the name with existing customer data already on file.

Consider the implications of two companies that are merging hoping to expand the customer base and reduce redundant processes. If both companies are selling multiple varieties of sweetened corn flakes, for example, the merged company can eliminate the redundant products and reformulate the existing ones and get the consumers from both of the original companies hooked on the "new and improved" sweetened corn flakes. In other words, at first a merger looks as though it will bring in the customers of both companies, maintain the revenue of both companies, and drastically reduce the operational costs of both companies. But what happens if it turns out that 50 percent of the cornflake eaters from both companies are actually the same customers (Figure 2.3)—they have just been buying both types of cornflakes all along (based on which one was on sale) when they did their weekly shopping?

The customer base has not doubled, nor has the revenue of the combined companies. They were customers all along—something that a due diligence sampling of merged data could have uncovered but only if the data was reliable and accurate and could be readily analyzed.

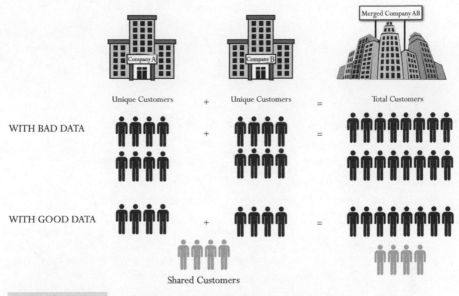

FIGURE 2.3   Bad data can lead you to think you have more customers than you really do. In the case of a merger, there could be shared customers of the companies being merged. Without knowing this beforehand, a merger won't achieve the financial gains that were expected.

Postacquisition issues raise a different set of risk mitigation problems that inaccurate data can complicate. A key reason an executive might sell stakeholders on a merger is to reduce redundancies. But this requires being able to quickly figure out what redundancies exist. I am not talking about merging data from disparate systems, but instead looking at issues like being able to compare Company A's parts list to Company B's parts list and creating a master list that can help the merged organization quickly figure out which parts or products are redundant.

As mentioned earlier in the chapter, reputational risk is as important  to mitigate as financial and regulatory risk. In mergers and acquisitions, reputational risk is very real—yet often overlooked. A large insurance provider was struggling to get a single view of each household as it grew through mergers and acquisitions. Without a single view of the customer across systems, the company had no easy way of identifying customers who held multiple policies with the company. Worse yet, they could not prevent mistakenly soliciting an individual who was already covered under a policy held by another member of the same household. Imagine how the customers felt when they received these solicitations and what affect it had on the company reputation.

As the *Information Age* survey referenced in Chapter 1 suggests,[3] risk mitigation is the most likely reason a company will pay attention to data quality. That may be thought of as a reactive posture, but there is a huge benefit to first choosing to tackle data quality to mitigate risk. Many risk mitigation projects are contained and specific. Yet they tend to require companies to integrate data from multiple applications and systems. They are ideal test cases for learning about the value of quality data.

Like the proverb that introduces this chapter, you can't completely mitigate risk. It will always exist. But with consistent, accurate, and trusted data, you'll be able to better identify and avoid most risk. And as an added benefit, your corporate information will be more transparent and give you the ability to run your business better.

■ NOTES

1. "French Bank Rocked by Rogue Trader," *Wall Street Journal*, January 25, 2008.
2. "Triple-A Failure," *New York Times*, April 27, 2008.
3. "Data Governance: Protecting and Exploiting a Key Business Asset," *Information Age* Research Report, Michelle Price, February 22, 2008.

CHAPTER 3

Controlling Costs with Accurate and Reliable Data

Beware of little expenses; a small leak will sink a great ship.

—BENJAMIN FRANKLIN

EXECUTIVE OVERVIEW

Are you making the most of your corporate expenditures? Estimates show that 10 to 20 percent of an organization's revenue is lost due to added expenses resulting from poor data management practices. A good data foundation impacts many different areas of cost control including:

- IT modernization
- Spend analysis
- Supply chain optimization
- Inventory management
- Order to cash optimization
- Marketing cost reduction
- Business process automation

Are your expenses where they need to be?

(continued)

(Continued)

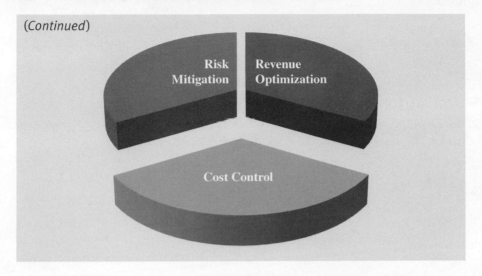

REMEMBER

1. Data quality and data governance should *never* be considered a one-time project. A quality culture must be established as an ongoing, continuous process.

2. No organization can tackle enterprise-wide data quality and data governance all at once. To be successful, your journey must be evolutionary. Start small and take achievable steps that can be measured along the way.

Similar to Benjamin Franklin's quote on page 31, most executives understand that small leaks can damage their company. The most difficult task, however, is figuring out where the leaks are, plugging them, and doing it all before the ship sinks. Just as we saw with risk mitigation, data quality plays a huge role in cost control. Data quality can improve customer-facing efforts by eliminating duplicate records on customers across data sources. Or it can mean driving efficiencies in the supply chain by reconciling a chaotic view of inventory, parts, and services. With better data, any organization can find new ways to contain costs and achieve impressive return on investment (ROI). Solid data can also help manage human resources and inventory spending more efficiently.

Cost control, though, is not glamorous. Titles on controlling costs do not dominate the business bestseller list. And executives are unlikely to give the subject a great deal of attention unless an economic downturn hits. At that point, it is probably easiest to say "We are cutting 1,500 jobs" or "We are going to reduce raw material costs 10 percent" and let their staff handle the details.

I would like to make the case that executives should pay attention to the details—specifically how accurate and trusted data can enhance your cost control efforts and how incremental improvements in data management add up to big savings down the road without big expenses. If you need convincing, consider this nugget: A few years back The Data Warehousing Institute estimated data quality problems were costing U.S. businesses over $600 billion a year.[1]

The economy swings up and down—and economic downturns force companies to think outside the box in order to stay viable for 10, 20, or 30 years down the road. Downturns disrupt business as usual. Ian Charlesworth, practice leader with Ovum Software, the global IT analysis company, believes the disruption means companies need to stop looking at their data as just a collection of stuff sitting on computers. "The real problem," says Charlesworth, "is that we don't know how to value our data. During the industrial revolution the key assets were machinery and warehouses. In the *information age*, it's people and data. Companies need to know what data they have, where it is and how to access it." That is never truer than in the arena of cost control.[2]

Organizations struggle with the most basic of cost analysis—just understanding what they are spending money on. Few organizations dig further into costs to not only understand their spending but also to optimize it. You are spending money on employees, raw materials, and services. You are paying taxes and levies. You have transportation and shipping costs. You spend money to communicate with your customers. You spend money on infrastructure. The list goes on and on.

Managing your spend may be one of the quickest ways to improve your company's bottom line. In this chapter I am going to address ways to manage costs with better data. The examples range from getting addresses right for marketing and billing purposes to properly coding supply purchases for spend management. I will look at how data quality can keep major enterprise resource planning implementations from becoming major money pits. None of these examples require a wholesale re-engineering of your IT department, your systems, or your solutions. Each example is an opportunity to see how incremental improvements in data management can make a huge difference.

How Accurate Data Plays a Role in Controlling Costs

Government postal services have spent hundreds of years trying to stream-line address systems to deliver the mail faster and more accurately. And, as we all know, mail still does not always make it to its intended recipient the first time. Something as benign as dropping the "North" or "South" off an address can send a letter to postal limbo. Undoubtedly, inaccurate addresses cost companies billions of dollars. With better data, any company can quickly reduce costs by getting bills and marketing materials to the right addresses of their customers.

One of the first areas that data quality software was widely deployed was in the mail order catalog business. A decade ago it was not uncommon for your household to get multiple copies of the same catalog—one with your name and one with your name plus the middle initial and maybe a third with just your first two initials. Data quality software has dramatically re-duced that practice. And while companies usually do not think of cost con-trol as being something that improves their relationship with the customer, something as seemingly small as getting the address right has that neat side effect. Customers appreciate it when they are not bombarded with market-ing materials. On the flip side, customers' opinion of your company does not exactly improve when they get a past due notice—despite never re-ceiving the original bill because it was mailed to the incorrect address.

And while address cleanup has made its mark, organizations do not save nearly as much as they could. Sometimes, it is because organizations out-source mailing activity to firms that are supposed to maintain clean lists but have no financial incentive, since they are paid by the piece. Other times, organizations take the view that cleaning up the data is sort of like removing leaves from the storm gutters—doing it once every year or two should suffice.

Here is a typical example. A global leader in online le-gal, business, and news information was using an outside vendor to mail 12 million pieces for more than 2,000 yearly campaigns. Duplicate names and invalid addresses led to numerous issues like sending prospect solicitations to law firms that were already existing customers. After a data quality initiative, the company estimated it saved $1 million from reduced outsourcing and mailing costs. With clean data, the company was able to successfully analyze its customer base and personalize its marketing messages.

Bill collection is another area that benefits tremendously from clean, accurate data. Sending a bill to the wrong address or to the wrong person at a company, will invariably slow down the time it takes to collect. The financial ramifications multiply for every wrong address. Say you bill customers for $1 million worth of work per month and 25 percent of your accounts receivable mailing list is inaccurate. That means, perhaps $250,000 is coming in later than expected. If you have to borrow money to pay expenses while you wait to be paid, you are losing money. And that is before the cost of remailing the inaccurate bills, and dealing with irate customers with a late fee for a bill they never received.

Getting data in order can create tremendous cost savings in terms of employee hours spent dealing with data problems. One unit of one international oil producer installed a data quality program that dramatically reduced the amount of time it took to analyze and understand corporate data. This same company also used data quality to get a better handle on the people it employed and what each employee did. As crazy as it sounds, the head of human resources (HR) did not know how many employees the company had because it had a unique HR system for each of the 120 countries where it did business—an amazing 120 disparate systems! An employee in one country that reported to a supervisor in another country would show up in the old data as more than one employee. Now, each employee has a master record and HR has a better understanding of the people it employs and what each one costs. The HR executive can now do some strategic planning, asking questions like "Which job categories will be impacted by retirements in the next five years?" and "Which areas of the world have the highest concentration of in-demand specialists?"

Personnel costs are particularly important to understand and control during economically difficult times. If a line of business does not know who its employees are and what they are contributing, how can executives make coherent decisions on a workforce reduction? Personnel is the biggest expense most companies have, but choosing a standard "15 percent across the board layoff" approach could lead to cuts in the wrong department or the loss of critical personnel. That risks depressing sales and profit further. With better data, companies may find they do not need to cut as deeply as they thought. Verification of your basic business rules can also help you control employee costs. For example, you may define salary grades for your employees. A particular salary grade—call them Level 13s—can earn between $90,000 and $120,000 annually. Do you have an automated way of discovering if any of those Level 13s are earning more than that? Accurate data can render powerful cost savings in ensuring you are not overpaying based on job classification.

MANAGING YOUR SUPPLY CHAIN BY UNDERSTANDING WHAT YOU ARE BUYING

Another problem many organizations experience is that they cannot figure out how much they are spending on products and services. The problem seems simple enough, but even comparatively small businesses struggle getting a 360° view of spend. Companies invest in spend analysis, supply chain optimization, and business process automation solutions. But the promise of efficient cost containment has not quite been delivered.

The reason is simple: Human individuals (that is, your customers or your employees) are relatively easy to classify. With address, e-mail, phone, and name data, you can segment them for efficient marketing or understand where they fit in the organization chart. The products and services you buy to sustain your business are more complicated to categorize. Take the light bulb. What is the wattage? Is it fluorescent? Tinted? Energy efficient? People will classify the same light bulb 100 different ways (see Figure 3.1).

To reduce spend, organizations turn to supply chain and enterprise resource tools. But instead of solving the procurement managers' problems, these cost control solutions complicate matters. Enterprise resource planning (ERP), supply chain management (SCM), and other applications encapsulate the processes that drive a business every day, yet they typically have no integrated data quality capabilities to find and eliminate unreliable data. Creating additional ERP or SCM applications on top of existing applications—which essentially develops redundant silos of product information—turns the task into a Gordian knot. Duplicate product numbers, obsolete product IDs, and inconsistent item descriptions exist across the organization. While this may have a positive impact on one aspect at the

How are your products classified?

"100 Watt"   "Tinted"   "Energy Efficient"   "Fluorescent"

FIGURE 3.1   **Product Classification, Lightbulb: Employees see products differently and classify them in unique ways. This can lead to the same product being classified in four different ways.**

operational level, the overall impact is an inability to understand the products that are being sold, and the raw material purchases needed to make those products. This can affect the organization's ability to plan for production changes, to get the best deal from their suppliers, to have the right inventory on hand, and to plan new products in the future. Similarly, a confused, disparate view of direct and indirect spending can foil the most well-intentioned spend management efforts. Production and distribution efficiency starts with consistent, accurate, and reliable purchase and supplier data. The bottom line is that poor-quality product data makes it impossible to control the costs of production, the productivity of the company, and the delivery of finished goods. So, how do we cope with all of these problems?

Companies have increasingly embraced industry-standard commodity coding systems like UNSPSC (United Nations Standards Products and Services Codes) and eCl@ss to provide a vendor-neutral, objective way of classifying data that tries to drive out human subjectivity. A standard code, when applied to a product or inventory item, can be used as a way to reference and sort this data across any application. For example, within UNSPSC, the code 31151806 represents a standard commodity description and meaning that can be used in every organization (in this case "laminated wire"). With this code appended to the record, every organization supporting this code can compare prices between various laminated wire suppliers more effectively. Or a company can reconcile every product data entry within their applications that has the 31151806 code and begin to see how much the company is spending on that type of product. These standards are a way of acknowledging that product data can—and will—have unique representations within the systems. By providing a single, universal method for classifying that information, the data quality problems inherent in product data will provide organizations with an understanding of what products they purchase and what suppliers they utilize.

A large aerospace company was struggling with a million unique item records—and to compound the problem, the company was adding 10,000 to 20,000 additional item records each month. A substantial number of these records were similar or identical to items being bought elsewhere in the company. The company knew it had vast amounts of duplicate data and conflicting data for the same items, but did not know which data was problematic. As a result, the company could not successfully track product logistics across different parts of the organization.

The aerospace giant had started sending data to a third-party vendor—at a significant cost—for coding. It took eight weeks to get the data correctly coded, and the company was charged per record—something executives found expensive and inefficient. It also suspected the vendor was not always reducing duplication. In fact, a spot check found one product had been coded under 121 unique classifications.

Through commodity coding and standards-based technology, the company was able to bring the coding process in-house with an automated solution that cost about half of what a single year's worth of outsourced data processing cost. Processed data is now available immediately, instead of after an eight-week delay. And the automation rooted out the multiple errors coded in by the vendor.

Cost control is critical to any company's success, and the solutions that power supply chain optimization, automated business process, and spend analysis are growing increasingly useful. Although you can purchase cost control solutions with every bell and whistle attached, you will not hear a sound if the data feeding these systems is inconsistent and inaccurate.

CONTAINING COSTS IN THE SUPPLY CHAIN

Containing costs in the supply chain is impossible without sound data. Here are the steps companies need to take to address product data quality:

- **Analyze the Data.** Use data profiling or data discovery to uncover strengths and weaknesses in the data. Determine whether there are duplications or if the data lacks standards across systems.

- **Improve the Data.** Address the known problems in the data through automated standardization, verification, matching, clustering, and enrichment practices. If you don't have a standard product classification definition, choose a vendor-neutral coding system like UNSPSC (United Nations Standards Products and Services Codes) or eCl@ss.

- **Set Data Controls.** Since new data is continually streaming into the organization, apply monitoring techniques to find and flag bad, suspicious, or noncompliant information *before* it enters your systems. It is important to remember that data is not static and that problems can creep into data for any number of reasons, including both human and machine error.

THE GOLD STANDARDS IN PRODUCT STANDARDIZATION

Product standardization efforts are similar in concept to the Library of Congress Classification (LCC) system for books. There are defined chief standardization and classification protocols: protocols like UNSPSC, the eCl@ss system, and GS1. These are multitier classification hierarchies that describe products and services and their attributes. Each code has both the same commodity description and meaning for every organization. Data quality

(Continued)

technology can map the organization's internal product definitions into a classification code common across the entire organization. With this code appended to the record, every organization
supporting this code can compare prices between various suppliers more effectively. Or a company can reconcile every product
data entry within their applications and apply the appropriate
code number and begin to see how much the company is spending on that type of product.

UNSPSC is a 10-year-old effort. The current version of the code
can be found online. Members gain access to previous versions of
the code and can help shape the code's future. eCl@ss is a mem-
ber-supported effort that is popular in Europe and has more
detailed product searching capabilities.

This same practice of mapping products into hierarchies is as
applicable to the management of finished product catalogs as it is
to the management of supply chain and materials management.
Often, these hierarchies are proprietary hierarchies that reflect the
organizations. Manufacturers and retailers are often faced with
providing customers and consumers with easy ways to navigate
the products and services they provide. Only by having a consistent classification system can they provide an easy navigation system based on the attributes of the products and services. Consider
the Web site of your local hardware store. Is it easy to navigate the
products and product characteristics in a fashion that makes
sense and provides the appropriate product choices? If so, it is
because they have mapped all of their finished products to a hierarchy based on common navigation requirements.

USING CLEAN DATA TO BETTER CONTROL INVENTORY COSTS

Just-in-time inventory is a well-documented business practice that is hard
to pull off with any real cost savings if the underlying data is chaotic. While
a finished product will have a single stock-keeping unit number (SKU),
there can be hundreds of parts rolled up into this single product, and each
of these parts will also have their own SKUs. And to make it more complicated, each of these parts can have subparts with their own SKUs, while the

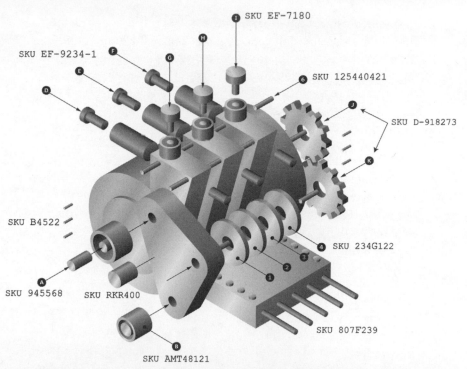

SKU EF-7180

SKU EF-9234-1

SKU 125440421

SKU D-918273

SKU B4522

SKU 234G122

SKU 945568   SKU RKR400

SKU 807F239

SKU AMT48121

FIGURE 3.2   **When SKUs Attack: A finished product can be made up of multiple components, each with its own SKU, dimensions and descriptions. Managing these parts in an inventory management system is challenging without consistent data.**

raw materials at the base of this product hierarchy will have their own unique identifiers (Figure 3.2). Complicating matters, each part or raw material could have an array of dimensions (for instance, weight, height, material, color, position, and so on) or other information describing the part or material—dimensions or descriptions that could run for pages.

A finished product may be unique in itself, but it is likely that many of the parts and materials making up this finished product are also used in other finished products. This means that any data quality issues with a particular part do not affect just one finished product. In fact, data quality problems can reverberate throughout the company's finished products, creating problems in areas such as usage and reporting, inventories, cost control, product development, product launch, and customer service.

Modern manufacturing organizations understand just how important it is to manage the inventory of parts used in finished products. If the right materials are not in place when they are needed, the production process grinds to a halt. An efficient inventory strategy requires organizations to have the right raw material on hand at the right time. Otherwise, just-in-time becomes way-too-late. Moving commodities from one facility to another or having to shut down product lines because materials are not available costs organizations in terms of productivity and efficiency. Storing commodities, raw materials, and finished products costs money—money that could be spent improving the business. In order to achieve this just-in-time inventory, manufacturers must know what materials they have, where those materials are, the ability of suppliers to deliver, and the requirements of each production facility. In most organizations today, this information is kept in many application databases, using different product coding mechanisms. Most organizations have little understanding of their total purchasing with a single vendor and have little knowledge of their suppliers' ability to deliver. The key to solving these problems is in the data.

It is not just manufacturers that struggle with data-driven supply chain issues. Data problems emerge across the marketplace because there are different coding standards within an industry, and a company does not necessarily choose a systematic way to deal with those conflicting standards. One example is a large book chain that was struggling to get the right product to its shelves. The problems resulted in the simple fact that they had too many systems and too many coding "standards." Their product data at the store was managed by SKU number, at the warehouse they used UPC numbers, and when they ordered books from publishers they used ISBN (International Standard Book Number) codes. As if three separate coding systems were not enough, certain departments at this book chain would override portions of the UPC codes, and individual departments would discard another department's coding numbers. Eventually, the company's inventory management and supply chain broke down. The individual book stores would try to order books using one set of codes only to be told the warehouse did not have that book. Meanwhile, the book was sitting in the warehouse unsold and the shelves at the store remained empty.

I will never forget the look on the business users' faces when they came to talk to me after days of deep discussions with the IT department. When they saw a report that featured UPC codes, the classification system IT *thought* the business users worked with, they were shocked. "That is not our data," the business users exclaimed. They were right because someone was overwriting the UPC codes with misinformation resulting in an inability to get the right product on the shelves. After cleaning up their UPC coding and developing a mapping scheme for the SKU-to-UPC-to-ISBN translation, their inventory was better managed, and their supply chain began functioning again.

EXACERBATING THE PROBLEMS WITH RFID

Radio frequency identification (RFID) can offer benefits in terms of ensuring consistent and accurate product data. RFID allows a product or a container to "identify itself" by broadcasting over radio waves what it is. But like ERP, SCM, and commodity coding systems, RFID by itself cannot cleanse data, and it cannot ensure that data errors of some sort are not in the data that is transmitted from company to company. If fact, RFID can introduce errors into an organization. Sensors pick up the wrong signal, signals are captured multiple times, and RFID signals do not sync with product database encoding standards. In these cases, some of the very virtues of RFID—high-speed, high-volume transfer—can have disastrous effects on a company. If the data being transferred is of poor quality, RFID can actually speed the process of contaminating the quality of the company's data. RFID is just one more source of data but you need to provide the same rigor and practices to RFID data as you do any product data.

WHY REDUCING YOUR APPLICATIONS WILL NOT MAKE YOUR DATA PROBLEMS GO AWAY

By this point in reading this chapter you might be thinking, "Weren't all these data problems going to be eliminated by reducing the number of solutions we have and putting everything on an enterprise-wide platform?" Not necessarily. A fresh coat of paint can do wonders for a house, unless the painter slaps the coat over rotting trim or a mildewed surface. Likewise, reducing the number of applications you use to save money could end up costing more if data quality is not addressed. Data quality solutions are the primer and trim you need before you decide to fix up your data house by reducing the number of applications containing critical data. Standardizing on enterprise applications, such as ERP and SCM, offers few real benefits in terms of data quality other than the illusion of data consistency and accuracy. Even when standardizing, few companies have only one source and system of data, either internally or externally. As a result, there is a good chance that problematic data is going to worm its way into a company. Furthermore, these applications are not designed to correct data errors, but remarkably their overall success or usefulness is dependent on high quality data. When populated with poor quality data, even the best ERP system will deliver useless results.

 An executive at a global paper manufacturer described the situation a few years back at his company. "At the time, we had one of everything," meaning that the company had almost every commonly used ERP package in use somewhere in the enterprise. Dozens of business applications each contained unique data, tailored for a specific business unit or area. Sound familiar? The company wanted to achieve a global, enterprise-wide view and decided to consolidate to one ERP system. But this company knew that simply dumping all its data from dozens of systems into one would not solve its problems; it would just create more errors. After implementing a data quality solution that could be embedded into its ERP migration, it was able to standardize product data across geographic regions.

 Large-scale data migration and consolidation projects are notorious for running over budget and beyond anticipated schedules. Often, bad data pollutes the system, requiring massive rework and reloading of data during the implementation process. Additionally, end users become frustrated with new software if the underlying data is not useful or accurate. A Midwestern energy utility had the foresight to build in data quality at the beginning of a multiyear project to standardize all its ERP systems on a single SAP application. The project involved hundreds of IT and business employees. By making data quality a priority from the beginning, this utility company met or exceeded budgetary targets and time schedules throughout the implementation.

Not every organization will decide to standardize all data across one platform. In fact, in most cases, to maximize the benefits of an enterprise-wide application, it is necessary to integrate with other existing applications to increase process integration and share core master and transaction data across the enterprise. Therefore, a critical success factor when implementing an ERP system, or a similar application, is to not just focus on the packaged applications, but also to make sure that data quality and data integration are managed in order to yield the maximum return on investment. Without data quality and data integration, business processes will still be plagued by defects caused by inability to eradicate data errors, and an inability to integrate, consolidate, share, and synchronize core operational data, master data, and historical analytical data across the enterprise.

 Sometimes data needs to be cleaned as a company makes the transition to a systemwide ERP. Nalco Co., a water systems and processing company based in Naperville, Illinois, is like many organizations that have acquired other companies whose data cannot immediately be integrated into the company's existing SAP platform. Gaps between the non-SAP and SAP system can lead to things like "hanging orders" where demand side never gets an order or two records are created so a customer gets double-billed. Nalco implemented a data cleansing initiative to stop that from happening. Once it has all of the company on its SAP platform it will continue to use data cleansing to keep its information accurate.

 Making sure data is correct is particularly critical in some venues, such as government agencies dealing with payments to citizens. Government is under pressure to control costs, but if the upshot of cost control efforts in the application arena is an increase in costs because the data is faulty—the government takes a double hit. A European government agency is currently working on a project to merge three separate government pension programs into one Oracle-based social security establishment in a multiyear process. The country had a separate pension system for laborers and white-collar workers and another system for government, teaching, and academic employees.

The cost savings make the merger a good decision for taxpayers, but it also comes with high stakes. The goal is to create one pension record for each individual. In implementing the new system, the government must make sure that each citizen's file offers the right credits under the previous systems and—going forward—the correct credits under the new, joint system. Inaccuracies and duplications could result in duplicate checks to some individuals and smaller or no pension checks to others.

PUTTING DATA AT THE FOREFRONT OF YOUR COST CONTAINMENT EFFORTS

The success of any cost containment initiative your organization undergoes is predicated on the quality of the underlying data. Whether you are in the midst of a multimillion-dollar merger, or simply trying to pare your marketing expenses, the data's cleanliness will make or break the success of the project. Despite that, the quality of the data is often considered as an afterthought and the costs associated with poor quality end up hidden in the hours that employees spend manually fixing up address lists or dealing with irate customers. It is registered on the faces of supply chain and inventory managers who are not getting the ROI they expected from enterprise solutions. It impacts sales as orders are lost, items do not make it to shelves in a timely fashion, and customers are frustrated that your company cannot provide the appropriate service. Clients often ask me for a concrete way to measure ROI. Unfortunately, the ROI calculations are not as straightforward as you might hope. What I can tell you about ROI: You might not ever know the ROI, because it is so difficult to benchmark how much poor data is currently costing you. I will tell you that getting your data in order will only cost you a fraction of the merger you are undergoing, or the supply chain ERP you are introducing. It will be a lot cheaper than outsourcing your mailing list or billing problems. I often recommend that companies start a quality initiative with one basic project, because once the validation comes in, other departments and divisions will be demanding a similar solution.

■ NOTES

1. Wayne W. Eckerson, "Data Quality and the Bottom Line: Achieving Business Success through a Commitment to High Quality Data," The Data Warehousing Institute (2002).
2. "Data Governance: Protecting and exploiting a key business asset," *Information Age* Research Report, Michelle Price, February 22, 2008.

CHAPTER 4

Optimizing Revenue with Quality Data

It is a capital mistake to theorize before one has data.

—ARTHUR CONAN DOYLE
(VIA SHERLOCK HOLMES)

EXECUTIVE OVERVIEW

Organizations run on revenue. This is true for government, nonprofit, and commercial organizations alike. In order to maximize your revenue, you must know your citizens, donors, or customers. You have to know what they want and do not want. It is all in the data. Data impacts all aspects of revenue, including:

- Customer loyalty
- Customer churn
- Customer acquisition
- Competitive advantage
- Reaction to marketing changes
- Corporate innovation

(continued)

(*Continued*)

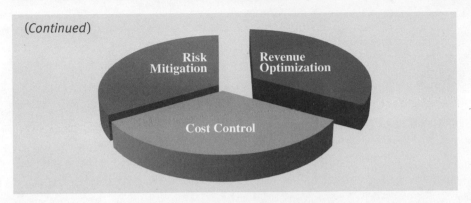

REMEMBER

1. Data quality and data governance should *never* be considered a one-time project. A quality culture must be established as an ongoing, continuous process.

2. No organization can tackle enterprise-wide data quality and data governance all at once. To be successful, your journey must be evolutionary. Start small and take achievable steps that can be measured along the way.

In the effort to improve revenue and profits, companies increasingly study their relationship with consumers. Who buys from us? What do they buy? What marketing efforts trigger greater spending? Who are our most profitable customers?

While companies are engaging in customer relationship management (CRM) and similar solutions to answer those questions, they are also trying to enhance revenue through programs like revenue optimization and yield management solutions. CRM focuses on the trees. Revenue optimization and yield management focus on the forest. All require sound data.

> CRM focuses on the trees. Revenue optimization and yield management focus on the forest. All require sound data.

Let's talk about CRM first. CRM helps companies use data to recreate the kind of one-on-one relationship that small businesses had with their customers 50 or 60 years ago. Given that customers have so many more choices than they had a half-century ago, understanding the customer is critical to driving sales. "It all comes down to the consumer's demand to marketers—know me or my loyalty drops to zero," says Peter Harvey, CEO of Intellidyn, an information and analytics service provider that I have had the pleasure to work with.

You cannot just know what the customer buys—or likes to buy. You need to know how valuable a customer is. A customer who buys all her sporting goods at your store, regardless of whether the item is on sale or not, is more valuable than the one that only purchases when there is a sale or coupon. CRM allows you to know who buys what products and services, as well as when they buy them, and ultimately, why they buy them.

Many CRM deployments, and other similar solutions, get derailed by inadequate data quality processes. These applications are filled with inconsistent, inaccurate, or unreliable data. At the same time, the CRM system is rarely the only system of record for customer data—customer information is usually found in different applications in marketing, sales, finance, distribution, support, and call centers. Data quality and data integration capabilities help companies aggregate this information, taking data from the CRM system and other systems to build a master record of each customer. With one master record of the customer, rather than a dozen conflicting records, companies can improve customer outreach, enhance customer retention, and maximize resources.

Revenue management and optimization programs that attempt to price products for maximum return can also be hamstrung by inadequate data. Hotels, for example, price rooms based on supply of different types of rooms as well as demand for those types of rooms. Knowing the customer room requirements is not enough. If a hotel chain does not know how many rooms are available with king beds rather than double or single beds, an effort to manage and maximize the price of each type of room is doomed.

If your customer data is stored in multiple, inaccessible locations, you need help—a bridge of some sort—for the data to be useful. A quarter of respondents to a Ventana Research[1] survey said they have customer data stored in more than 20 systems. Sometimes, companies are not even aware of the gold mine they have sitting in one of their information silos. For instance, a company's CRM system could be set up to track coupons sent to customers. Meanwhile, data from company-issued rewards cards could be sitting unused in a different silo. The data, together, could provide much more targeted and timely offerings. It is no wonder that the majority of CRM-related projects fail to do what businesses hope they will do. Even when companies can get a single view of the customer across multiple data channels, they frequently have data that is inaccurate, out-of-date, or duplicated. More than 40 percent of companies take on CRM or similar projects without understanding data quality problems in existing systems.[2] Another substantial hurdle is that two percent of data becomes out of date each month because of death, divorce, marriage, and relocation.[3] If your company has 500,000 customers and two percent of the records become obsolete each month, 120,000 of your records will be out of date within a year.

The people in your company who work with data know this. Only 11 percent of respondents to the Ventana Research Survey have full confidence in their data. As is the case with business users who focus on supply chain, inventory, and purchasing, those focused on customer issues will cobble together data from multiple sources, load it into a spreadsheet, and create their own version of the truth—the kind that changes as the spreadsheets get e-mailed from user to user.

When faced with inaccurate data that does not reflect your business, revenue optimization through better customer knowledge is difficult to achieve. It is also difficult to measure results, or make sure that efforts to boost revenue were not, in fact, undermining it. For example, a retailer gave out choice discount coupons to "frequent shoppers" only to discover, after a better integration of customer data, that a portion of those frequent shoppers returned a substantial portion of the products they bought, costing the retailer more money to process the returns and reshelf the inventory than they were making on their "frequent shoppers." Only by merging and rationalizing information from multiple systems were they able to understand the buying patterns of these shoppers. This was only possible with quality data.

SMALL FIXES EQUAL BIG REWARDS

Here is a great example of how a simple process like eliminating duplication can achieve tremendous results. Pitt Ohio Express is a Pittsburgh-based freight service company that ships throughout the Mid-Atlantic and Great Lakes regions. With 22 terminals in its service area, Pitt Ohio makes over 9,500 daily deliveries to more than 14,000 locations. Like so many companies, Pitt Ohio keeps multiple databases. Sales reps would enter information into a marketing contact database while the company maintained a transactional database with details on each shipment. The transactional database emphasized speed over precision as it was critical to expedite customers' freight on the 10,000 invoices generated daily.[4] However, the marketing database needed accurate information to be useful.

Further complicating matters is that customers do not always provide the address in quite the same way. For example, they might put a return address as the company's post office box on one day. Another day, they might use the physical street address. Compounding the difficulty is the fact that there can be multiple addresses, mail drops, and post office boxes all within the same company. Organizations' names may also appear differently—such as CT&T, CTT, and CT&T Corp.

Pitt Ohio frequently ended up with multiple records for the same customer. Add the customer name and address confusion to an outdated data warehouse that got purged only once every six months, and it is easy to see why the company received a lot of returned mail. Meanwhile, because of the unreliable customer database, the marketing folks threw up their hands at the possibility of providing a targeted program. The problems reached a critical point when Pitt Ohio's owner asked how many customers the company had and no one could find an accurate answer. It had 650,000 customer records but no real answer for how many actual customers that represented.

An effort to solve the duplication problem using a spreadsheet program failed due to lack of matching and merging capabilities. Additionally, the process was slow and prone to errors. Desperate for a better way, Pitt Ohio turned to data quality technology. The company now has consolidated information for each customer that helps it keep track of things like the best contact people and how they like to be contacted. Instead of the one-size-fits-all campaigns of previous years, the company can now create customized campaigns based on purchasing behaviors and geography. One recent campaign pushed purchases of premier services by 20 percent.

 Not only do you need to know how many customers you have, it is important to know how they found you so that you know how to find more of them. That was the case for an Internet-based insurance company that pulls quotes for consumers from numerous insurance providers. The company works with hundreds of different Web sites to drive customers to its quote service. In some cases, customers might find their Web site via one of its partners and request a quote on car insurance. The same customer might come back another time, going directly to the Web site, and request a quote on homeowners' insurance. Before the company began using data quality technology, that same customer would have been considered two different customers. Now, the company can instantly match a customer's record to previous site visits. This allows the company to better serve its customers, market its services, and choose its advertising partners.

ACHIEVING A 360° VIEW OF THE CUSTOMER

Let's talk, for a moment, about reaching that Holy Grail—the 360° view of the customer that is constantly up to date. The minute a customer interacts with your company—orders clothing, books a hotel room, schedules a service visit—your system should not only tell you who the customer is, but it should also tell you if a special price or offer is appropriate. Obviously, this requires a coherent internal data management strategy. But do we know everything about customers from their interactions with us? Certainly not. For additional customer information, you can buy or lease data from other sources—credit data, geographic data, and government data. And once you open your internal systems to outside data, it does not matter how well-organized those systems are or how well-maintained you systems are—the systems are not going to automatically integrate. External data is the skunk at the picnic, threatening to wreak havoc. At this point, you need some type of internal solution for acquiring and sorting through data. You must apply your own quality and business rules to align the external data to match your view of the customer.

 For a major resort company, the challenge was to integrate external data in a view that reflected a household and not the individuals in it. Let's use the Smith family to illustrate how a 360° view of the customer can benefit an organization. In a six-month period, both Mr. and Mrs. Smith booked a vacation and charged it to their personal credit cards. Mr. Smith handled the summer beach trip, and Mrs. Smith took care of the winter ski trip. Even though these appear to be two separate entities in the data the resort company purchases, the reality is that a single household is taking these vacations.

The resort company needed a household view that incorporated its own data from reservations with external data. And it wanted all the data—external and internal—organized by household. And because revenue optimization is tough to pull off when the data is weeks or months old, it wanted the data to exist in real time. You might ask why clean, real-time data is so important. Say Mr. Smith booked and cancelled three ski vacations in a three-week period. And then Mrs. Smith books the fourth trip the following week. The company wants to know this—at the moment Mrs. Smith books—so that she does not receive quite the enticing deal her husband got the first time he booked. After all, this family has cost the resort money by tying up reservation agents and rooms without the resort earning a dime.

 Here is a different take on achieving a 360° view, or as the Cintas Corporation calls it, "One Customer." Cintas rents, leases, sells, and cleans uniforms around the world. It also provides services like clean entry mats, towels, fire and safety protection items and resources for clean rooms. Many Cintas customers are franchises, parts of chains or branches of government bodies like school districts and state governments. For Cintas, a "household" might be a grouping of all the restaurants in the same chain in one greater metropolitan area.

With its multiple services and products, Cintas sales representatives have a great many cross-sell opportunities that the company thought it might be losing because it did not have one view of its customers. Different products and services were managed by different lines of business with different databases and sales and marketing systems. Cintas knew they could provide better support and services for their customers. But, since the systems were not integrated, they didn't know what customers had what products. It was difficult to answer questions like: "What is the true amount of business a customer does with Cintas?". The company also felt it could not promote existing relationships to customers and prospects effectively. And then there were the flat-out data errors that crept into databases, like this entry for an address: "Go around the back of the building."

By improving its data, Cintas has been able to prioritize prospecting and to improve national and major account compensation accuracy. All of its efforts now drive revenue optimization.

BETTING YOUR BUSINESS ON SOUND DATA

I make the case throughout this book that every company needs to pay attention to its data. Well, maybe that's not entirely true. If you are so small you know all of your customers, every last one of your suppliers, have no regulatory burdens, and do not keep much inventory, you can probably get away with manually fixing your data problems. Most companies, however, do not fall into this category. Most companies are data-intensive, and their reputation with customers will simply fall apart if they do not pay fastidious attention to their data quality.

 One of these companies is Intellidyn. As head of an information and analytic services company, Peter Harvey has staked his company's success on creating some of the largest databases in the United States that integrate credit, demographic, lifestyle, property, and auto ownership and purchase behavior. These databases fuel the company's offerings in list services, analytics, database marketing, data management, and strategic consulting. Peter's advice to clients: "You know [your customers] by their transactions. When you can show consumers that you know them, it is amazing what happens in terms of loyalty and renewals, which drives profitability."

Intellidyn pulls in data from automated bank machine transactions, voice response units (VRU), call-center activity, Web site hits, and purchase transactions as well as most major credit unions. It models and scores on close to a real-time basis. Unlike companies that control the inputting of company data through ERP systems, Intellidyn is working almost exclusively with data generated outside the company. To assure the best data within its databases, Intellidyn incorporated data quality and management into its IT structure. They have reported back impressive results. Clients now have access to a reliable view of their customers within hours instead of days or weeks.

OPTIMIZING REVENUE THROUGH EFFICIENCY

 Many companies go through dramatic growth periods that bring in plenty of revenue and profit but also tax their existing systems to such a degree that it is hard to sustain the growth. Sometimes the groups processing all the new sales go begging for extra help, when what they really need is better data. BMC Software was going through something similar. The world's seventh-largest software provider offers enterprise management solutions that help organizations make the most effective use of enterprise-wide systems, applications, database and service management. BMC has pioneered the development of business service management to help customers better manage IT from a business perspective. This business has boomed in recent years.

BMC deployed a sales force management tool that was not being used consistently enough by its sales force. After implementing a data quality methodology, the company's sales force began using the tool more effectively. "We cleaned up the data. We solidified it. We changed the views of the sales force and they have become more efficient. It has had a ripple effect. It did not just help sales. When we started rolling this out, the order management people started saying 'Wow!'" explains Bruce Castner, Director of Customer Operations and Data Quality. The end-of-the-month crunch—when sales were being processed—was not the time-consuming, burn-the-midnight-oil event it had been previously, because the processors were not getting hung up on issues like address and customer information inaccuracies. Speaking about the month-end close, Bruce explains about his co-workers in collections: "They have come back to us and said 'Whatever you are doing, It is great!'" This is a great example of how quality data management can provide numerous advantages as it propagates throughout your organization.

Whether it is getting an address right, building a 360° view of a customer, bringing in outside data to better understand customers, or optimizing the solutions designed to optimize your revenue, the whole process is built on a platform of accurate, accessible data. Like cost containment, revenue optimization does not require sweeping IT changes or significant purchases to achieve incremental ROI. And, these changes can bring fast rewards. Companies are rarely successful when they say, "Okay, we're going to fix every bit of data in one fell swoop." More often, successful companies say, "I want to improve this one area," and when they see the results, they roll out the process to other areas of the company. It did not take a day to build those silos. They cannot be bridged nor torn down in one day.

MAKING REVENUE MANAGEMENT FUNCTION EFFECTIVELY

Revenue optimization and yield management are critical strategies for many economic sectors. Pioneered by the airlines who sought to maximize profitability in the postregulation world by examining limited, perishable resources (airline seats), predicting consumer behavior, and adjusting prices accordingly, the practice has spread to other sectors with perishable goods from grocery stores to hotels. But to successfully use revenue optimization and yield management software, companies have to make sure the data flowing into these systems is accurate.

Here is a simple example: Let's look at a fictional, big box retailer: Shop-O-Rama. Its sales are boosted each year by certain seasonal events, among them back-to-school and holiday shopping. Prior to each school year, Shop-O-Rama slashes prices on the back-to-school items, like lunchboxes and backpacks. Since school systems start at different times of the year, area managers are asked to input information on local school starting dates. If an area manager enters an incorrect starting date— "010908" instead of the correct "090108"—the yield management software will not be able to pick an effective date to slash the merchandise to half-price. As a result, Shop-O-Rama will miss the maximum revenue generation period that is fueled by sales, and it will be stuck with a pile of action figure–themed backpacks and notebooks that will be hard to sell after school begins.

Predictive forecasting solutions will fail miserably if the data feeding the forecasts is inaccurate. Continuing my previous example, another big sales driver for Shop-O-Rama is the holiday season. Prediction of holiday sales must be done carefully since the merchandise has a short shelf life. Looking at trends from the previous year, Shop-O-Rama concludes that people must be buying more linens at the holidays, as there appears to have been a huge upswing. However, the reality is that because of poor data entry, holiday-themed towels were entered twice last year—once under "holiday merchandise" and again under "linens." When the holiday season comes and goes and the shelves are still full of holiday linens, management is left to figure out what went wrong. And what to do with all those linen Santa Claus–decorated toilet paper cozies?

So Many Solutions, So Much Potential for Failure

Arthur Conan Doyle's success as a writer stemmed from the way his main character, Sherlock Holmes, used deduction and logic to solve crimes. Holmes could draw large conclusions from small observations. But Holmes's world was comparatively small. Some knowledge of geology, anatomy, botany, and law helped him solve cases. Our organizations are too large for any one person to be able to do the deductions necessary to beat the competition to market with a new product or understand the different customer bases. But just as Holmes' creator said, we need data before we can make any decisions.

And that data needs to be consistent, accurate, and reliable.

VALUE OF CLEAN DATA TO NONPROFIT ORGANIZATIONS

Britain has a single-payer health system, but it does not cover everything. For one London-based research institute, fundraising is critical to the success of its mission. The hospital's fundraising arm wanted a unified view of its donations database. The charity knew it had lots of duplicates and inaccuracies. With the help of data quality improvements, the organization improved the accuracy of its 3.5 million financial records it held on more than 500,000 donors. It has been able to investigate data held on donors by geographic and socioeconomic categories. This information provides a clear representation of a donor's likely level of contribution, allowing for targeted fundraising in geographic areas where the hospital's charity has a low penetration.

WHAT'S NEXT?

In this first part, I have discussed the business case for sound data management and data quality. It should now be apparent that there is a direct correlation between the quality of your data and the health of your business. There are many case studies and examples of organizations that have felt the impact of data on their business. Some of these examples may directly reflect your organization, some may not. You may not even have seen your organization reflected in any of the case studies. But, you can bet that the success of your organization is highly dependent on the quality of your data.

This entire book is a guide to assessing and managing your data to ensure that it reflects the needs of your organization. Achieving this level of success requires a concentrated effort. Any major effort in an organization requires funding and executive buy-in. This first part should have provided a foundation for building a business case. Any business case for better data should be centered on the advantage to the organization. Stressing risk mitigation, additional revenue generation, cost reduction, or customer relationship improvement will give you the foundation to secure corporate buy-in and participation.

What I have reiterated throughout Part One are the two fundamental ideas about data management: (1) it is not something that you can do once and be finished, and (2) you cannot address all data quality issues at once. Better data requires you to have a culture of quality. That culture requires a different way of thinking and working. It requires attention to people, processes, and technology, and adjustments and optimizations to each of these. In the next part I will help you assess your use of people, process, and technology, and help you map out the next steps for a data quality culture in your organization.

Data must be treated as a corporate asset. You must provide the funding, staffing, and attention that you provide to other assets in your organization. If you look at the way your organization treats data today, would you say that it is properly funded, staffed, and managed? Would you say that it is easy to produce reliable and trusted data for reports that drive decision making? Probably not. Let's move on to Part Two and discover how you can treat your data as a corporate asset and begin your journey to becoming an optimized and governed organization.

■ NOTES

1. Ventana Research, "Customer Information Management: Business and Technology Trends" (2007).
2. Gartner, Inc. "CRM Demands Data Cleansing." Ted Friedman, et al., December 3, 2004.
3. "Data Quality and the Bottom Line: Achieving Business Success through a Commitment to High Quality Data," The Data Warehousing Institute, Report Series 2002.
4. Data Integration Helps Pitt Ohio Express Get to Know Its Customers, June 9, 2008.

The Data Governance Maturity Model

CHAPTER 5

Governing Your Data

It takes a long time to bring excellence to maturity.

—Titus Livy, Roman Historian

Executive Overview

In Part Two I will take a look at how to determine the data governance maturity of an organization. Understanding the maturity of an organization is the first step in determining the next steps to take on the road to managing data for success. To help guide us through organizational maturity, I will use the Data Governance Maturity Model. The model is explained in detail throughout this part. At a high level, the model identifies an organization's data management practices as being undisciplined, reactive, proactive, or governed based on technology adoption and business capabilities.

The goal of this part is to provide information that will help you classify your organization and help you determine the best approach forward. As organizations elevate their data governance maturity, they reap the rewards of being a better managed business, rewards such as:

- Increased revenue by better managing customers
- Reduced expenses by optimizing operational systems
- Optimized product delivery by better managing the supply chain

At the same time, increasing to a higher level of data maturity will reduce the risks in an organization, such as:

(continued)

63

(*Continued*)

- Compliance violations
- Customer churn
- Poor business decisions

But progressing up the maturity model is not easy. It requires a concerted effort at organizing your work force, at optimizing your business processes, and at the appropriate application of technology. Throughout this chapter, I will look at the people, process, and technology issues associated with each level of the maturity model to help you understand how your organization operates and to help you determine the best path forward.

Remember

1. Data quality and data governance should *never* be considered a one-time project. A quality culture must be established as an ongoing, continuous process.
2. No organization can tackle enterprise-wide data quality and data governance all at once. To be successful, your journey must be evolutionary. Start small and take achievable steps that can be measured along the way.

As you have read in Part One, a strong business case exists for increasing the quality of your data. Organizations rely on data to make significant decisions that can affect customer retention, supply chain efficiency, and regulatory compliance. In areas like demand forecasting, performance analysis, and market positioning, business intelligence has replaced—or at least supplemented—traditional methods such as gut feelings and experience. But as companies collect more and more information about their customers, products, suppliers, inventory, human capital, and finances, it becomes more difficult to accurately maintain that information in a usable, logical framework.

THE BUSINESS OF DATA QUALITY

The data management challenges facing today's business stem from the way that IT systems have evolved. Enterprise data is frequently held in disparate applications across multiple departments and geographies. The confusion caused by this disjointed network of applications leads to poor customer service, redundant marketing campaigns, inaccurate product shipments, risk exposure, and, ultimately, a higher cost of doing business.

Companies attempt to combat the spread of information silos by implementing enterprise-wide data governance programs. The ultimate goal is to codify and enforce best practices for data management across the organization. Meeting this goal can be frustrating and elusive. There is no manual that lays out a step-by-step plan, so the path can seem confusing and difficult to maneuver.

In Part One, I mentioned the need for organizations to have a framework that allows for the incremental improvement of data. This framework embraces new applications, optimizes existing systems, and retires legacy applications. All of these applications and solutions should be viewed through the lens of data quality. This framework is the Data Governance Maturity Model.

Every organization has unique issues and concerns. By using the framework of the Data Governance Maturity Model, you will have a roadmap that will get you started. If *data governance* is a term you are not familiar with, you are not alone (see Figure 5.1). Eight percent of companies surveyed by *Information Age*[1] in 2008 had never heard of the term. Another 22 percent said it was not on the company's agenda.

So, what is data governance? At its most basic it is a methodology or a philosophy for gathering, managing, and benefiting from your data. It is

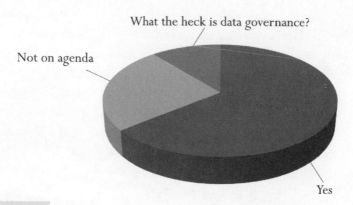

What the heck is data governance?

Not on agenda

Yes

FIGURE 5.1   Is data governance in your company's near-term future?

not a program. It is not a technology that will "fix" a problem. It is more than just having a strategy. Data governance is a mindset. It is about establishing a culture where quality data is achieved, maintained, valued, and used to drive the business.

In Part One, I outlined the business drivers for data governance with numerous case studies. Many of the companies I wrote about have a strategy— 42 percent of *Information Age* respondents said they do. However, a strategy, alone, is not enough. You need to assess how that strategy relates to the Data Governance Maturity Model. Through this model, organizations can identify and quantify precisely where they are—and where they want to go—in creating an environment that can deliver and sustain high-quality information.

In Part Two, I explore:

- The major issues surrounding building better data across the enterprise
- Ways to utilize existing people, business processes, and technology to achieve more effective data quality policies across multiple departments
- Methods to determine the maturity of an organization's data management capabilities to find a data governance strategy that best fits the organization

IMPACT OF HIGH QUALITY DATA

Do you recall the story from the first chapter of the plumbing manufacturer that experienced the devastating plant fire? The fire exposed the fact that the company had lots of data on its customers and products, but could not answer a critical question: What customers were expecting which products? This was because data had not been managed from the top down, but from the bottom up. Business units were only concerned with entering and tracking data to meet the needs of their specific departments. Sales knew what was sold, not what was delivered. The factory knew what it had manufactured. Accounting knew who owed money. The result for the enterprise was a buildup of redundant, inconsistent and often contradictory data that was housed in isolated departmental applications spread from one end of the organization to another. A question like "What is the average time from close of sale to receipt of payment?" required weeks of digging and produced misleading figures because data was not recorded consistently across the organization.

If data did not grow at a phenomenal rate, this might not be an issue, but trends indicate that corporate data will double every 72 hours by 2010. IDC estimates that the world will reach a zettabyte of data (that is a 1 with 21 zeroes after it) in 2010[2]—a tripling from the amount of data generated in 2007. Meanwhile, Gartner estimates that through 2011, 75 percent of organizations will experience significantly reduced revenue growth potential and increased costs due to the failure to introduce data quality assurance.[3]

The effect of this avalanche of bad data is stunning. Larry English, author and information quality pioneer, writes, "Process failure and information scrap and rework caused by defective information costs the United States alone $1.5 trillion or more."[4]

As the impact of poor-quality data was initially felt in customer information applications, data quality and data integration technologies were deployed to correct those specific applications by implementing data quality solely in a sales force automation system or a database marketing application. But applying the solutions locally does not solve the problem. Instead it leads to some silos containing consistent, accurate, and reliable data, while others are mired by inconsistencies. When organizations then seek to unify their data, this piecemeal approach falls apart, leaving data stranded and mistrusted in remote silos.

The benefits to a holistic approach are obvious; better data drives more effective decisions across every level of the organization. With a more unified view of the enterprise, managers and executives can create strategies that make the company more profitable. A successful enterprise strategy will encompass three main elements (see Figure 5.2).

1. **People.** Your organization needs executive sponsorship as well as an IT and business staff committed to working together. A CIO or compliance officer or anyone with broad responsibilities that reports directly to the CFO or CEO is a good choice for executive leadership, assuming that person understands the business and not just the technologies. Additionally, the executives need to appoint, empower and fund staff to execute the governance methodology managed by a data stewardship group.

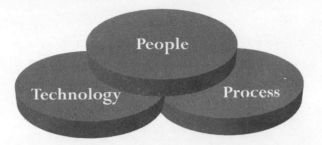

FIGURE 5.2   **Data governance embodies three components: the right technology, used by the right people, in the right business process**

2. **Process.** A data governance program must create and enforce what is considered acceptable data through the use of business policies that guide the collection and management of data. This has often been left to the IT department. But what is considered good, clean, usable data from a technical standpoint may not be complete, accurate, and timely information for the business user. A documented, repeatable process that is adhered to throughout the enterprise will ensure consistent data across your organization.

3. **Technology.** An effective data governance program requires technology: matching technology, data integration technology, data discovery, data synchronization technology, data models, collaboration tools, and other components that help create a coherent enterprise view.

REACHING BEYOND IT: WHY BUSINESS USERS MUST BE INVOLVED

IT has historically been both responsible for and the driver for such solutions as enterprise resource planning (ERP) and customer relationship management (CRM) systems. IT understood the underlying technologies and the potential they could deliver. IT did not, however, always understand how the business user interacts with these systems. While the installations of these systems were successful from a technical perspective, they often did not meet the needs of the business. So, IT got a bad rap. You have heard the story, the multimillion dollar ERP system was brought online, and business users grumbled that they could not get the data out of it, the data was inaccurate, or it made their life harder.

I think the origins of this problem stem from the fact that IT staff is often a bit interchangeable between industries, that IT staff is more concerned with the technology than with the business. A database manager for a retailer could easily get a job with a manufacturer. A systems analyst for a technology company could find work in a financial services company. Although industry specialization is becoming more common, IT staffers have typically not had to possess deep knowledge of the sector into which their organization falls. They also tend to work in an "IT Kingdom" (Figure 5.3), a mystical dimension where IT lives, but no one else in the

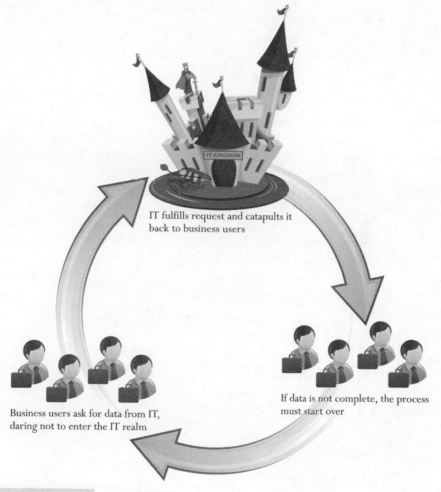

FIGURE 5.3   **When no one is allowed to enter the IT kingdom, requests for data and information are passed back without any business input**

organization dares to enter. Cross-functional teams consisting of IT and business users that are tasked with addressing data issues are sparse to non-existent. In addition, there have been times when IT has not helped its case by busily building up a fiefdom and selling executives on solutions like ERP, data warehouses, and CRM as grand problem solvers.

But let's not put the blame entirely on IT. As a matter of fact, IT some-times gets incorrectly blamed for the past sins of the company. IT has exe-cuted on the most efficient ways to solve tactical problems. This has always been a priority for IT. And, IT has done it with the tools available to them at the time. Sure, we are suffering because of these practices. But, that does not mean IT acted inappropriately or without the best interest of the orga-nization in mind. Business is changing and evolving. The structure of the past is insufficient for the needs of the future. "Data quality is perceived as an IT problem when it is, in reality, a business problem," notes Peter Harvey, CEO of Intellidyn, a company that helps organizations with data-driven marketing projects.

Today, it is not enough to execute effectively on a series of tactical problems. In order to be competitive—to innovate—an organization must work as a cohesive entity. This is forcing change. Good change. Organizations are starting to understand that they cannot just expect IT to put a solution in place. They need their IT staff

> Data quality is per-ceived as an IT problem when it is, in reality, a busi-ness problem.

to have specific domain expertise, whether it is pharmaceutical, finance, or manufacturing. Business users and IT need to work together, making sure that IT knows how the business works and that business users understand what IT can do to help them work more efficiently.

The need to work together—and what happens when groups do not—

can be illustrated by the example of the global retailer that had technical staff coding products one way and business users coding them another way. There are many ways to code products, services, and materials. These range from cross-industry standards to intra-industry standards to in-ternal company proprietary codes. Some typical standards include Stock-Keeping Units (SKUs), Universal Product Codes (UPCs) or European Article Numbers (EANs). For this global retailer, the product data at the retail store was managed by an SKU number. The warehouse used UPC codes. And since most of the products the company sold originated in Europe, Purchasing used EAN-13 numbers (the European equivalent of a UPC). From an IT perspective, everything was fine. The databases were populated, access was appropriately controlled, and the systems functioned to specifications. From the business perspective, things were in total disarray since there was no coherent way to determine the total products in the supply chain or the total products in stock.

This gap between IT and business users caused the retailer's inventory chain to break down. Once the groups bridged the gap and began to work together, stores could get the stock they needed when they needed it. But it was only possible once the business users detailed the supply chain problems to IT and IT worked with the existing systems to rationalize the product and stock information.

The Data Governance Maturity Model assumes IT and business users will learn to work together. If they cannot, an organization will not get beyond the undisciplined stage.

I have repeatedly discussed the idea that cleaning up your data is not a one-time effort. You are not overhauling the car—you are maintaining it. As Gartner puts it so succinctly, "To achieve such results, successful programs identify the organizational processes behind data quality. Much like regular IT housekeeping, from virus scanning or performance monitoring to data backup, the data quality program becomes part of daily IT routine."[5] Ultimately, though, the goal is more than just maintaining your data—the goal is improving your organization. But this improvement is only possible once the data management practices are robust enough to provide the data infrastructure your business requires for growth and improvement.

The Data Governance Maturity Model helps organizations understand their current level of data management, and, more important, the model can identify a path for growth in the future. While achieving a single, unified enterprise view is an evolutionary process, an organization's movement toward this ultimate goal invariably follows an understood and established path. In working with organizations over many years, patterns of data management practices have become clear. Based on these interactions, there are four stages to data

Stages of the Data Governance Maturity Model:
1. Undisciplined
2. Reactive
3. Proactive
4. Governed

governance maturity. While different parts of an organization can span the maturity levels, all organizations predominately fall into one stage or another. There are four distinct stages:

1. **Undisciplined.** Based on my experience with customers over the past decade, approximately 35 percent of companies fit this stage. These organizations are very tactical in the way they use their data and IT infrastructure. Often, they are in firefighting mode, putting out data quality brush fires while rarely seeing the big picture. Executives are not usually aware of the cost of poor data or the benefits of accurate data. There are no standards for cleaning and sharing data. Sometimes, a handful of individuals—usually IT personnel—are plugging holes in the data dikes, and if one of them leaves the company, the dike breaks.

2. **Reactive.** About 45 to 50 percent of organizations fall in this stage. Reactive organizations make an effort to fix data problems and typically have tools on hand to do so. However, the scope of issues is limited to a particular functional area or line of business. It is still common for groups to work independently with little executive oversight. There is a tendency in these companies to look only at short-range projects.

3. **Proactive.** About 10 percent of organizations have reached this level. Proactive organizations have executives who are beginning to view data as a strategic asset. The organizations have a data stewardship group and maintain corporate data definitions and business rules. Data is viewed from a corporate perspective and not a departmental point of view. Monitoring is ongoing, and goals shift from fixing problems to preventing them.

4. **Governed.** Governed organizations have executive sponsorship with direct C-level support. Data is a corporate asset, and data management is funded appropriately. Data is consistent across the enterprise. In return, executives have full confidence and trust in all data-based decisions. It sounds like data utopia and, indeed, less than five percent of organizations have reached the governed stage.

I cannot stress enough how important it is to identify the current stage of your organization's operation and to understand why you are at that stage. Companies that plan their evolution in a systematic fashion have an advantage over those that are forced to change by external events. The Data Governance Maturity Model can help control that change by determining what stage is appropriate for the business—and how and when to move to the next stage.

To get a better understanding of where your organization may fall on the Data Governance Maturity Model spectrum, take a look at Figure 5.4. The model shows the typical use of enterprise applications common in each of its four distinct stages. Each stage requires certain investments, both in internal resources and in technology. However, the rewards from a data governance program escalate while risks decrease as the organization progresses through each stage. The model also depicts the types of technologies where data consolidation and integration often occur. Initially, companies typically try to drive value from data within smaller projects (such as database marketing) and then move to larger projects. The stages of the model

> The Data Governance Maturity Model can help control change by determining what stage is appropriate for the business—and how and when to move to the next stage.

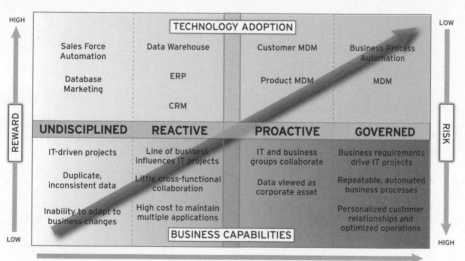

© Copyright DataFlux Corporation, LLC. All Rights Reserved.

FIGURE 5.4   The data governance maturity model

are a continuum, and movement from one level to the next will not happen all at once. There is also a chasm between the second and third stages, as organizations have found that the resources and commitment necessary to advance from the reactive stage to the proactive stage requires critical changes in executive support and corporate buy-in. I will describe this in more detail in later chapters.

At the end of the process, a company will have implemented a "single view of the enterprise," which leads to opportunities to integrate high-quality data with business process management (BPM) systems in order to automate business processes. At this level, organizations are using high-quality data to support the automation of routine activities that do not, or should not, require human intervention.

In the coming chapters, I will examine each stage of the model and explain how each of the following concepts should best be approached to maximize the effectiveness of your data governance initiative.

- **People.** Who is involved, and what contributions must they make? The best-functioning organizations understand that business issues should drive data governance and that IT plays a critical role in working with the business users.

- **Process.** What activities must be performed? What business rules must be available to properly govern data? What business processes will influence and be affected by the data governance methodology implementation. In undisciplined and reactive organizations, data is "owned" by a group. It is not governed by the organization at large and the concept of "sharing" data is rare. Proactive and governed organizations believe power derives from sharing information.

- **Technology.** What investments in technology are necessary? How should these investments be staged? Reaching a mature data state is not about replacing current systems and solutions, nor is it about buying one solution that will "solve" all problems. It is figuring out where you are and augmenting solutions to close critical gaps based on sound policies.

- **Risks and rewards.** What risks does the organization face at the current stage? And what could it gain from progressing forward? I am a firm believer in staging improvements, starting small, and taking matters one day at a time; all the while, realizing incremental advantages to your organization.

- **Advancing to the next stage.** What actions are required to move from one stage to the next? This is a particularly critical consideration for companies moving from the reactive stage to the proactive stage because it involves a bit of a culture change and the need to identify people with both business and IT experience to lead the data governance efforts. Even though data stewardship is a new concept for many organizations, the position of data steward is one that is becoming increasingly common and more likely to be funded. The data steward has the responsibility of building consensus across business units as well as working with IT to push the data policies out into the applications across the enterprise.

Along the way, I will share some examples of companies that have successfully made the leap from one stage to the next, and I will extract some key principles I believe helped them make the leap successfully. One of the most important things to keep in mind is that incremental change is good. It is valuable. There is no benefit in trying to rush this process or make a pronouncement that "we will go from the undisciplined stage to the governed stage in 18 months." In fact, if consultants tell you they will help you make that transformation in such a short period, show them to the exit—immediately. A more realistic view is to have portions of the enterprise at different stages. You could have groups that are still undisciplined, while others are moving into the reactive or proactive stages. In assessing your organization's maturity level, take into account the different stages and explore the best practices of the groups that are the furthest along on the maturity continuum. Assess the business drivers for change and concentrate on those business drivers that will provide the most benefit to your organization.

The governed stage is not a category that many organizations have yet achieved. And it is a category that will evolve as new technologies and new concepts come into play. It might seem a bit unachievable, but think of it this way: If your organization is struggling to make it to the proactive stage, you are not alone. Focus on achieving incremental goals before setting your sights on the governed stage. If you are stuck in the undisciplined stage, begin today to take the steps to achieve the reactive stage. You will be pleased with the rewards.

Remember: Data governance is an evolutionary process. It cannot be done overnight, or by next quarter, or in time for the annual meeting. It is a process that even the most mature companies strive to reach every day. But it can be done. And you can be the force to make it happen.

■ NOTES

1. "Data Governance: Protecting and exploiting a key business asset," *Information Age* Research Report, Michelle Price, February 22, 2008.
2. Lucas Mearian, "A Zettabyte by 2010: Corporate Data Grows Fiftyfold in Three Years," *ComputerWorld*, March 6, 2007.
3. Donald Feinberg, "Poor-Quality Data: The Sure Way to Lose Business and Attract Auditors," 2006.
4. Larry English, "Plain English about Information Quality: Information Quality Tipping Point," *DM Review,* July 2007.
5. Gartner, Inc, "Organizing for Data Quality," By Andreas Bittere, et, al., June 1, 2007.

CHAPTER 6

Undisciplined Organizations: Disasters Waiting to Happen

There is nothing so disobedient as an undisciplined mind, and there is nothing so obedient as a disciplined mind.

—SIDDHARTHA GAUTAMA, FOUNDER OF BUDDHISM

EXECUTIVE OVERVIEW

Characteristics of an Undisciplined Organization

- Think locally, act locally
- Few defined data rules and policies
- Redundant data found in different sources
- Little or no executive oversight

Technology Adoption

- Tactical applications to solve very specific problems: for example, sales force automation or database marketing
- Very localized data management technology implemented within the tactical applications, if at all

(Continued)

(*Continued*)

Business Capabilities

- IT-driven projects
- Duplicate, inconsistent data
- Inability to adapt to business changes

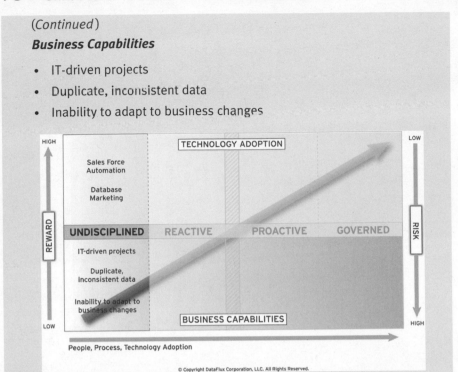

© Copyright DataFlux Corporation, LLC. All Rights Reserved.

Remember

1. Data quality and data governance should *never* be considered a one-time project. A quality culture must be established as an ongoing, continuous process.

2. No organization can tackle enterprise-wide data quality and data governance all at once. To be successful, your journey must be evolutionary. Start small and take achievable steps that can be measured along the way.

Business executives do not see themselves as undisciplined. That's why most leaders of organizations whose data maturity is undisciplined may not recognize their problem. Industry research has estimated that as many as one-third of companies are in this category, so there's a good chance your organization falls into this undisciplined stage. Do not panic. Take a deep breath and read on. The path from undisciplined to reactive is a clear one.

If you are at this stage in the Data Governance Maturity Model, your organization may look something like this: You have few defined rules and policies regarding data quality and data governance. The same data may exist in multiple applications, and redundant data is often found in different sources, formats, and records. There is little or no executive-level insight into the costs of bad or poorly integrated data. Sound familiar?

There are many large, successful organizations with undisciplined data management practices. This is both fortunate and unfortunate. It is fortunate because these organizations are successful. It is unfortunate, because it is only a matter of time before the poor data management practices will result in negative consequences—either in the form of increased risk or reduced benefit to the organization.

> Industry research estimates that one-third of companies are in this category, there's a good chance your organization is reflected in this undisciplined stage. Do not panic. Take a deep breath and read on. The path from undisciplined to reactive is a clear one.

The undisciplined organization typically finds out it has a problem only in a crisis: the fire at the plant of the plumbing manufacturer that revealed that no one knew if customers had been sent their products; or the rogue trader at Société Générale whose questionable trades cost the French bank $7 billion. It is not that these organizations were not keeping data. In the case of the plumbing manufacturer, the data was housed in separate silos. Figuring out which customers were owed what products involved a time-consuming, costly effort to match data on sales, product runs, and deliveries. In the case of Société Générale, the data may have been available, but it was only consolidated annually for compliance reporting.

One of the hallmarks of undisciplined companies is an absence of data standards and business rules—or even worse—a collection of conflicting data standards and business rules. One example is the secondary mortgage market company that had different rules for different lines of business. One division was authorized to buy mortgages that would be considered severely risky by another group. The lack of an enterprise-wide cohesive rule made it difficult for the organization to assess and manage its risks.

At Société Générale, the issue involved business rules. Quality data governance is not just about the accuracy of data but also about the ability to use it effectively to run and manage the business. The rogue trader's actions should have set off automated alarms within the bank's compliance department—alarms that couldn't be short-circuited through what was alleged to have been manipulation of the bank's computer systems. But since the proper business rules were able to be circumvented, the bank paid a high price for its failures.

What little data governance exists in an undisciplined organization is managed completely by IT. Since IT has little understanding of the business, this structure is certain to create an environment where the data does not reflect business needs.

WHEN NO ONE IS ON THE SAME PAGE

No two organizations are undisciplined for the same reason, but they often have some things in common. Chief among them are executive unawareness; minimal input from business users and business analysts; very few employees with any involvement in data; and data that is viewed as an "overhead" cost. It is a bill that needs to be paid, not a strategic asset. As you have learned so far, this is a recipe for disaster.

Somewhere, deep in the bowels of the company, an IT person has been tasked with managing the data that flows through his department. He may not even know the business analyst who uses the data that he is trying to maintain—or what that person needs the data for. But he is clued in to the need to keep it accurate. So, he monitors it regularly making sure there are no irregularities. However, if he leaves the company or moves to a different position, there is a strong likelihood that data quality will disintegrate. There is also a chance that more than one person is working on data quality—*but that they aren't going about it in the same way.*

Typically in undisciplined organizations there are individual groups that manage applications and data that are unconnected to the larger organization. Take the example of sales force automation tools. These wonderful tools are designed to keep customers from getting multiple sales pitches

> Why are organizations undisciplined?
> 1. Executive unawareness
> 2. Minimal input from business users and business analysts
> 3. Few employees involved in data
> 4. Data that is viewed as an overhead cost

from different people within the same organization, to increase productivity among sales people, to track sales leads, and to create sales forecasts.

Unfortunately, the success of the tool depends on accurate entries. If a salesperson in England enters "Lilly" for a company name, while a U.S. salesperson types in "Eli Lilly," the information will not show up in the same file. Many organizations have someone tasked with keeping the data accurate or establishing business rules for the entry of data. In an undisciplined organization, though, that person does not know about the data maintained in accounts receivable or by the marketing department. There is no opportunity to reconcile and fix data across the different silos. With these silos of unconnected data, a salesperson might not know that a customer is way behind on payment for previously purchased products. Sales may book and sell more products to this customer with no chance for future payment. This is just bad business. If the financial systems and the sales systems can't be synchronized, there is little or no confidence in revenue, sales, and pipeline reports. The CEO reporting revenue projections to Wall Street is flying blind.

What does the CEO do when the projections turn out to be wrong? In the undisciplined organization, the finger pointing is usually aimed at IT.

NONEXISTENT TECHNOLOGIES AND PROCESSES

Another characteristic of the typical undisciplined organization is that it does not invest in data profiling, analysis, or auditing of data. If anything is done, it is likely outsourced because undisciplined organizations figure managing data is the kind of thing you do "every once in a while," and can surely be handled less expensively by an outside company. With data, I do not ascribe to the theory that management gurus often preach: that companies ought to focus on what they do best—and outsource the rest. Your data is your business. Often organizations do not even vet the quality of the outsourcing. In Chapter 3, I referenced a company that outsourced commodity coding. They needed to do commodity coding in order to optimize logistics of parts and materials across their organization. The outsourcing company charged by the record, and it took about eight weeks to get the data back. Finally frustrated by the cost of outsourcing, the company brought the process in house with an automated system that cost half of a single year's worth of outsourcing and also rooted out multiple errors, including a commodity that was coded 121 different ways! Data is the life blood of an organization. It is a true competitive differentiator. Only you know your data. When it comes to your data, I encourage you to focus on the data as a critical part of your business. Focus on what you do best, but use your data to help sharpen that focus.

Policies tend to be made on the fly—if at all—in an undisciplined organization. It is common, for instance, for individual departments to have their own rules and processes for managing, organizing, and cleansing data. Decentralization may be good for some business practices, but data is not one of them. Data is typically kept in separate silos in an undisciplined organization. This causes a great deal of trouble for organizations that want to grow through cross- and up-selling. Figure 6.1 shows a typical telecommunications provider that offers land, wireless, and Internet service. Each entity keeps its own data, but gets credit for selling additional services. But the entities' data is not synched, so the organization does not understand the true value of a customer. With poor synchronization across the lines of business, the company is missing multiple, good opportunities

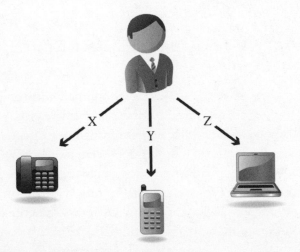

FIGURE 6.1   Unless some sharing of data across each of these telecommunications divisions occurs, it is impossible to know the true value of each customer. Meanwhile, customers may be contacted by a particular division that does not know they are already customers of another division.

for cross-selling. Or, worse yet, the customer could be bombarded with mailers for "new" services that she already has.

If data quality is addressed at all in an undisciplined company, it is done in response to a problem. Maybe a business analyst is able to mine the appropriate data to show that one reason delinquent accounts have increased is because the cross- and up-selling offers were made—and accepted—by clients barely able to pay for services they already had. But this is found out *after the fact*.

Once the problems emerge, the search for scapegoats is on, although the wisest executives quickly figure out there is no one person or group of people to blame because the process is broken. Usually at this stage, companies recognize problems with data integrity (but only at the departmental or business unit level) and begin to quantify the effects of poor data quality in the organization. When this recognition spurs change, the organization can reach a higher level of maturity.

> No one person or group of people [are] to blame for data integrity problems if the process is broken.

MAKING THE MOVE TO THE NEXT LEVEL

Undisciplined companies often make the move to the reactive stage after a significant failure. Examples include customer churn or perhaps a reaction to external demands such as compliance regulations. Faced with a reaction to events, undisciplined organizations want to move to the next level. They should begin by defining a process for evolving through the various maturity stages. To move to the reactive stage, a company must establish objectives for data governance, starting with an initial assessment that establishes a baseline for data maturity across the enterprise. Transitioning requires organizations to identify the size and scope of data governance efforts (for instance, is it a grassroots effort, or is there executive sponsorship?). Also, before moving to the next level, organizations should determine the critical data assets (customer, product, and so on) that will be involved.

The technology components that support this growth must be able to handle data quality and data integration tasks for cross-functional teams. More sophisticated data profiling, standardization, and verification capabilities provide a way to refine information across departmental boundaries. In addition, the ability to centralize business rules for core data quality functions in a single repository—and use those same rules across applications—is a critical element that facilitates growth.

To get your organization moving from the undisciplined stage, start with a data quality audit. Hire a consultant or purchase a data profiling tool to help you get an understanding of the data that exists across the silos in your organization. Begin to understand the relationships across those silos. Identify the anomalies and inconsistencies. Only then can you begin to plan for change. And remember, get the business users involved in this exercise, because only they know the true needs, and meaning, of the data.

Finally, after learning the results of an audit, companies should select one manageable project employing data cleansing and deduplication. It is possible a department within the organization has already done this. Database marketing teams often understand the value of accurate data. Ask about what they have done, and see where else that technique could be applied. If you take this methodical approach, one project will lead to the next, and you will advance to the next maturity stage level before you know it. There is no big bang theory at work here. Take it one step at a time based on business priorities.

ORGANIZATIONAL ROLES

Groups within an organization play different, yet critical, roles in helping companies reach further into the maturity model.

Executives: Executives need to be aware of the role data plays in helping companies reduce waste, improve customer retention, comply with regulations, and, ultimately, make the company more profitable. Executives need to ask how and where data is kept, how it is updated, and whether it is continuously cleaned or deduplicated. Executives need to understand if data is shared across the organization or kept in individual departments.

IT: The IT staff needs to understand the business—and help evangelize the need for consistent cross-organizational data. First they need to understand who needs data and how they use it. IT can sleuth out data needs and wants and evangelize the benefits of keeping one set of trusted data easily accessible to all business units. IT can help choose technologies that benefit business users.

Business Users: Business users need to understand how the data they need and the data they use fit into the bigger picture. A buyer for a retailer needs to understand how her selections impact the store planners and the forecasters. Business users need to convey to IT and executives the importance of getting accurate, timely data. They also need to understand the need—and potential—for cross-organizational data. This concept makes business users nervous as they want to own their data. But data-savvy organizations aren't about owning the data.

CHAPTER 7

Reactive Organizations: Trying to Get Beyond Crisis Mode

Man is not imprisoned by habit. Great changes in him can be wrought by crisis—once that crisis can be recognized and understood.

—NORMAN COUSINS, 20TH CENTURY MAGAZINE EDITOR

EXECUTIVE OVERVIEW

Characteristics of a Reactive Organization

- Think globally, act locally
- Presence of data management technology, but with limited data quality deployment
- Siloed data leading to many views of what should be the same data
- Awareness of data problems only after a crisis occurs

Technology Adoption

- Data warehouse
- Enterprise resource planning (ERP)
- Customer relationship management (CRM)
- Data integration tools

(Continued)

(Continued)

Business Capabilities

- Line of business influences IT projects
- Little cross-functional collaboration
- High cost to maintain multiple applications

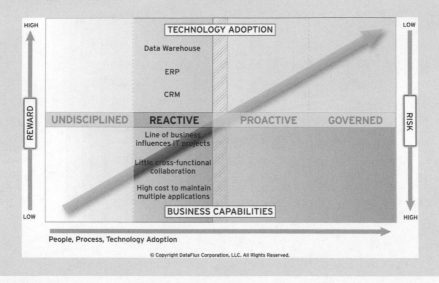

© Copyright DataFlux Corporation, LLC. All Rights Reserved.

REMEMBER

1. Data quality and data governance should *never* be considered a one-time project. A quality culture must be established as an ongoing, continuous process.

2. No organization can tackle enterprise-wide data quality and data governance all at once. To be successful, your journey must be evolutionary. Start small and take achievable steps that can be measured along the way.

Have you ever had one of those jobs where you thought, *If I can just get ahead of this crisis, things will really turn around and it will be smooth sailing?* From a data standpoint, that describes the reactive organization. Reactive organizations are aware of their data troubles, and they want to get them under control. But that control remains elusive.

Oftentimes, the deployment of an enterprise resource planning (ERP) or customer relationship management (CRM) solution triggers the realization of the organization's underlying data weaknesses. These systems are supposed to make a hugely positive change in the company and when they do not, it is usually because of inaccurate, unintegrated, or duplicate data. Executives at reactive organizations understand the full blame for the problems should not always be laid at the feet of the IT team. Still, it is sometimes less mentally exhausting just to point the finger and tell IT to fix it.

A reactive organization may actually be a mix of business units that are undisciplined, reactive, and proactive. Those proactive units, who have invested financial and intellectual resources into data quality and reaped some rewards, want to go farther. They are interested in establishing master data management (MDM) and business process automation (BPA) solutions to benefit from the personalized customer relationships and optimized operations that such solutions provide. They are also stuck in a difficult position, though. MDM or BPA processes cannot be fully exploited until the *entire* organization has at least reached the proactive stage. I have worked with companies that have tried, only to have been forced to table the projects until their company implemented sound governance policies and cleaned up their data across the organization.

PREPARING THE REACTIVE ORGANIZATION FOR MDM AND BPA

MASTER DATA MANAGEMENT

When the only computing companies did was on a mainframe, the goal was to have a master file. With distributed networks and solutions, many companies have gotten away from having one master file. MDM seeks to return to that concept—without losing the flexibility of distributed computing and solutions specific to different business units. In a nutshell, MDM is intended to support an organization's business needs by providing access to consistent views of the uniquely identifiable master data entities across the operational application infrastructure.[1] It is the "single view of the customer" that we have discussed throughout the book, but the concept of

(Continued)

MDM does not pertain just to customers—it is also relevant for *any* critical data domain, such as products, suppliers, or employees.

BUSINESS PROCESS AUTOMATION

BPA does what its name suggests. It automates processes to automate decision making, optimize processes, and reduce costs. The automation can be simple: scheduling clerks to work in a grocery store based on the busiest time of day. Or it can be more sophisticated: choosing how much merchandise to send to individual stores based on forecasting tools. Regardless of the complexity of its use, automation fails when the data underlying it cannot be trusted. For instance, if the grocery store does not have accurate data on the peak store hours or if it does not have the correct information on the hourly salary of the people it is scheduling, it could end up spending—and wasting—more money. If the retailer has duplicate or misaligned coding of past sales, an automated system could end up sending inventory that is redundant to the inventory already in stock at the store.

Organizations in the reactive stage are changing processes, responsibilities, and technologies to prepare themselves for the proactive stage. At the same time, these changes are improving the daily execution of the business requirements. As these organizations implement data management practices to improve the cross-functional communications of processes and applications, they are preparing the groundwork for MDM and BPA. Localized benefits will quickly evolve into cross-functional benefits and ultimately to cross-organizational benefits.

I have discussed the importance of executive sponsorship in creating a mature data governance approach several times throughout this book. The reactive organization is often at a crossroads in this regard. There is awareness in the C-suite of the critical role data plays. It is likely that the CIO is fairly tuned in to the strengths and weaknesses of different business units and their data. But this issue has not quite hit the dashboards of other executives—yet. Data management is seen as sort of a side item—something to address after this quarter's revenues are shored up or costs are controlled.

DEFINING THE REACTIVE ORGANIZATION

A reactive organization will usually locate and confront data-centric problems only after they occur. The ERP, CRM, or data warehouse applications perform their assigned tasks, with varying levels of data quality. While certain employees understand the importance of high-quality information, corporate management support is lacking or incomplete. In the organizations that I have worked with, about 50 percent today are reactive in nature.

> In the organizations that I have worked with, about 50 percent today are reactive in nature.

I call these organizations reactive because they tend to react to data issues only when they find themselves in a crisis. The good news is that reactive organizations are asking the hard questions:

- Why am I losing market share?
- What are my best-selling products?
- Is my organization meeting regulatory compliance requirements?

And, more important, reactive organizations understand that the answers to the questions are in their data—but only if their data is managed in a more consolidated fashion—rationalized across systems and departments.

So, when a reactive organization is losing customers or market share—they turn to data to try and figure out what is happening. They begin to realize the data is not helping them spot the underlying trend before it turns into a crisis. Maybe they are trying to answer the question "Why am I losing customers?" Part of the reason is that information from the disparate systems used by the call center, finance, sales, and marketing are completely out of sync. Sales does not know about the complaints to the call center, while marketing is touting a new-and-improved solution, all the while remaining oblivious to the struggle the service side is having to support it. When the situation is viewed from a 10,000-foot perspective, it is easy to see how misaligned data can lead to lost customers.

A reactive organization will struggle to meet regulatory compliance requirements. Regulatory compliance is a typical problem that moves an organization forward in the maturity model. Regulatory compliance, by definition, must encompass the entire organization rather than just a single application or department. This type of initiative is the start of corporate data governance.

Reactive organizations are now evolving in that they have begun to operate across functional areas and lines of business. They realize the best way to answer the difficult questions and react to mounting pressures is to require and get cooperation from different parts of the organization. This is an important step forward. Reactive organizations find success when a group of database administrators or other capable and skilled employees—such as data-savvy business users—create data quality programs and join together to determine consistent business rules across parts of the business.

Like undisciplined organizations, reactive ones allow individuals to create useful processes for data quality initiatives without any standard procedures existing across the enterprise. The good news, though, is that standards begin to take shape across functional areas. Unfortunately, the good news ends there. While the problem may have crossed the radar screen, there is usually very little corporate management buy-in to an enterprise-wide approach to data quality or data integration.

People are not immune either. Reactive organizations risk losing their smartest data managers when those individuals become frustrated by the lack of attention paid to data quality issues and choose to join organizations that are more responsive. Without a data champion, ad hoc groups of employees are left to create rules for data quality and data governance. With an emphasis on correcting data issues *as they occur* instead of *before they happen*, there is not much time to create cross-system rules. Most data management processes are short-range and focus on recently discovered problems. Unlike the undisciplined organization, roles and tasks within a business unit or department are usually defined.

Like the companies in the undisciplined stage, organizations in the reactive stage have a lack or conflicting collection of business rules. This handcuffs the company because it limits the ability to assess and manage risk. Reactive organizations usually have a limited arsenal of data quality tools available, and individual business units have access to them. But like the cross-system business rules, the company often uses them only after they discover a problem.

It is also likely that any currently installed CRM, ERP, or data warehouse solutions use data quality or business rule validation technologies in a limited and isolated fashion. Despite the inherent promise in CRM and ERP solutions for cross-functional data, most data is not integrated across business units. Some departments attempt isolated integration efforts. For instance, accounts receivable might try to create a more direct link with distribution. Data is still seen as something that department and business units want to control. Reactive organizations have plenty of employees who do not believe what the "official" data says. They keep their own spreadsheets that get passed around the department, tweaked and fixed along the way until it is hard to keep track of how many versions of the truth are floating around. These are the organizations where finance and marketing will vehemently disagree on the cost and benefits of a specific project—each waving a different set of numbers in the others' faces. Often, these organizations know what went wrong two months ago, but do not know how to make things right today.

To combat these issues, organizations begin to monitor data quality and business rules adherence in a methodical fashion—but it is typically a reactive process. If we look again at the issues around regulatory compliance, organizations are trying to move from laborious and manual exercises to generate compliance reports for every reporting period. Reactive organizations can spend an entire reporting period getting ready for the next round of reports. With the inclusion of monitoring capabilities, the problems of data rationalization can be reduced as the data is appropriately monitored for problems and rectified on an ongoing basis. As organizations mature to late-stage reactive and early-stage proactive, monitoring becomes a standard practice—these organizations strive to find problems before they enter the organization and damage the business.

The risks for organizations in the reactive phase are high. There is a lot of data in these organizations. What elevates the risk level is that so much of it is inconsistent and unintegrated. While data is analyzed and corrected sporadically, data failures still occur on a cross-functional basis. What successes these companies achieve come from individuals heroically going against the grain to create processes that work in individual business units. Sadly, these people are rarely recognized for their work.

I have discussed the failures of ERP, CRM, and data warehouse systems in a reactive organization. This is a huge frustration with executives who were sold on the idea that these systems would solve all their data problems. I would imagine some of you are wondering whether these investments were worth it. I can testify they definitely were. This data quality discussion would not even be relevant if you were not gathering this data to begin with. The power of these solutions brings the need for better managing the data into sharp focus. Your goal should now be to get the most out of your investment by governing your data properly.

HOW TO TELL WHEN YOUR COMPANY IS READY FOR THE PROACTIVE STAGE AND MDM

It is as important to understand when you are ready for a data leap as when you are not. One customer that embraced the Data Governance Maturity Model is a large nonprofit organization headquartered in the United States. The organization wanted to build a more unified view of its donor network, whose data was splintered in dozens of applications across the country. The IT department decided on an MDM program and began to seek technology vendors to support the effort.

The organization found that although its intentions were good, the people and processes were not ready for that move. Political battles broke out to determine who owned the data. No single group was responsible for determining what constituted a good record. The bare necessities of data governance were not in place, and initial trials were gridlocked.

Once the organization understood that it was an undisciplined company according to the maturity model, it had a plan to progress to the next level. Business analysts within the company used data profiling technology to identify bad or incomplete data. The management team established a data stewardship group, which started to codify business rules for data quality and data integration efforts. Within months, the organization had progressed to the reactive stage—and the goals of MDM were now within reach.

MAKING THE MOVE TO THE PROACTIVE STAGE

Moving from the reactive stage to the proactive stage is probably the most difficult leap to make, despite the potential return on investment (ROI). This is the point when organizations need to stop thinking as individual business units and start working together. The move to the proactive stage requires managers and executives—from both business and IT—to work together to create new, strategic visions for correcting and consolidating data. The process cannot be driven exclusively by IT. Business units that are accustomed to maintaining their own applications and data structures may find it difficult to embrace a more corporate view of the data governance strategy. As a result, progressing to the next stage requires a high degree of executive support—and a resulting culture shift—to create the unified, proactive view of the organization.

Once a vision and strategy have been established, the move to the proactive stage requires the creation of a data governance team (sponsors, stakeholders, domain experts, and data stewards). This team—particularly the data stewards responsible for day-to-day oversight of the data quality procedures—establish cross-functional business rules that correspond to preidentified levels of data integrity. Cross-functional business rules are critical to move to the proactive stage. For instance, human resources may code employees by pay grade. However, a project manager, putting together a budget for a project, may use an hourly rate. As pay grades are generally less specific than hourly rates, the numbers will not be the same, creating conflict as to how much it really costs to run a unit. Another example involves creating business rules for valuing customers. For a financial services organization, if one unit segments customers based on how much they keep in their accounts, while another unit strictly rates customers on how much it makes from issued credit cards—there is no overall value number. Instead, there are multiple values for each customer floating around the organization. If another part of the organization—for example, the home equity unit—wants to figure out whom to market to, it will not have a clear picture of the customer. Or worse yet, the home equity unit may extend credit to customers that should not be approved. From the technology side, data quality and data integration capabilities become a core component of the cross-enterprise IT platform. The organization is more reliant on service-oriented architecture (SOA) to tie data management processes to operational applications, making data quality a critical component of any system.

Finally, companies moving to the proactive stage should use data monitoring technologies to uncover substandard data *before* it causes problems. Despite the fact that moving from the reactive stage to the proactive stage involves the dismantling of business unit information silos and a strong commitment to cross-functional data, this progress is not an all-or-nothing proposition. Again, I will stress the need to take data management one step at a time. As you move your organization into the proactive stage, look at individual silos and think about how they can be grouped with another silo. If there is more than one solution driving the supply chain, focus on integrating the data of those systems. A financial institution can start by pulling all compliance-related activities into a single unified data master. A retailer might focus on getting sales, store planning and forecasting linked. Instead of nine silos, you move down to four. And then from four, you move down to two, until finally, you have the single version that reflects your entire business. Analyze how that process worked, how much better the company is doing because of it, and move on from there.

■ NOTE

1. David Loshin, *Master Data Management*, page 9.
2. The Morgan Kaufmann Publishers, Copyright 2009 by Elsevier Inc., Burlington, MA.

CHAPTER 8

Proactive Organizations: Reducing Risk, Avoiding Uncertainty

Proactive people aren't pushy. They're smart, they're value driven, they read reality, they know what's needed.

—STEPHEN R. COVEY, *THE SEVEN HABITS OF HIGHLY EFFECTIVE PEOPLE*

EXECUTIVE OVERVIEW

Characteristics of a Proactive Organization

- Think globally, act collectively
- Mastered use of enterprise resource planning (ERP), customer relationship management (CRM), and data warehouse technology
- Executives who view data as a strategic asset

Technology Adoption

- Customer master data management (MDM)
- Product MDM

(Continued)

(Continued)

- Employing enterprise-wide data definitions and business rules
- Enabling service-oriented architecture (SOA) architecture for cross-organization data consistency

Business Capabilities

- IT and business groups collaborate
- Enterprise view of certain domains
- Data viewed as a corporate asset

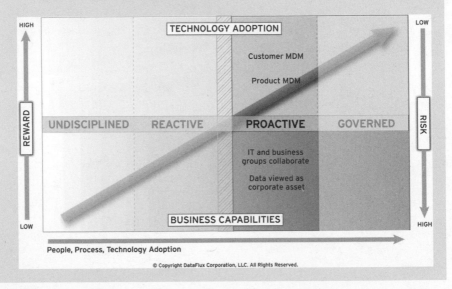

© Copyright DataFlux Corporation, LLC. All Rights Reserved.

REMEMBER

1. Data quality and data governance should *never* be considered a one-time project. A quality culture must be established as an ongoing, continuous process.

2. No organization can tackle enterprise-wide data quality and data governance all at once. To be successful, your journey must be evolutionary. Start small and take achievable steps that can be measured along the way.

In the proactive organization, data is treated as a corporate asset. This means that it is appropriately funded, sufficiently staffed, and has visibility at the executive level. Proactive organizations regularly analyze their data to segment customers, improve their supply chains, lower their costs, forecast sales trends and provide all-around better decision making.

Proactive organizations have executive sponsorship on data issues; have a single view of their customer, product, or other valuable data assets; and are poised to implement automated processes that save more money and further free up the organization's staff for strategic planning.

> In the proactive organization, data is treated as a corporate asset.

Proactive organizations have graduated from fighting fires, arguing over the usability of data and building siloed fortresses of data unavailable outside of specific business units. These organizations have mastered their use of customer relationship management (CRM) and/or enterprise resource planning (ERP) technology. Not surprisingly, only about 10 percent of companies worldwide have reached this level.

I have talked a lot about the need for cross-functional, organizational-wide data, but just gathering this data and dropping it into a warehouse that is accessible to business users across the enterprise does not qualify your organization for the proactive stage. These organizations are forward-looking in that they take a domain-specific approach to data through master data management (MDM) technologies that group data to look specifically at a data type such as customer, product, supplier, or asset. This approach effectively provides consistent data across operational as well as analytic/data warehouse environments. Retail or financial services companies have all their data centralized around customers. Manufacturers or distributors might initially take a product-centric approach. This is a huge improvement over the reactive organization, and as I will discuss in Chapter 9, it is another key stepping stone to becoming a truly governed organization.

Moving to the proactive stage is the most difficult transition for an organization to make. Oddly enough, though, it is not the technology that is the difficult part. It is the people, the politics, and the behavioral shifts that are required that make the proactive stage difficult to reach. In the proactive stage, there is a requirement for consistent data and business rules across the organization. These are difficult to achieve. People that are not used to working together have to put aside their differences and agree on the best way to represent the organization through the data. It sounds simple enough to make sure the data reflects the business, but it is not. Very basic concepts are viewed differently across the organization. Getting agreement across lines of business and functional areas is difficult. These difficulties make the evolution to the proactive stage hard to achieve. But the rewards are well worth the effort.

When Data Governance Becomes Important

At this level, management understands and appreciates the role of data governance, and commits personnel and resources to data efforts. Executive-level decision makers view data as a strategic corporate asset. Key among the personnel resources is the selection and deployment of data stewards. These individuals protect the *integrity* of the data and work directly with cross-functional teams to enact data quality standards and consistency.

DATA STEWARDS: THE SUPERMEN (AND SUPERWOMEN) OF YOUR DATA INITIATIVE

I have touched upon the role of data stewards in previous chapters. These individuals are critical to the success of any data governance project. But who makes the best data steward? Is it a position you can hire from outside the company? Can you hire a consultant to assume the role and then teach internal people to take over?

Let's talk first about who makes the best data steward. I like to think of these people as being multilingual. But rather than knowing, say, Spanish and English, they know technology and business needs. The data steward is the central point for communicating across different lines of business, someone who understands the needs of business analysts and IT and can articulate those needs. A data steward is either an IT person who is business savvy or a business person who is IT savvy. You need someone in the role with an investment in the quality of the data and an understanding of the potential return on investment (ROI).

As you get your data governance project up and running, remember that there will be more than one data steward in your organization. A data steward has a very direct responsibility with a line of business. It is the responsibility of the data steward to ensure that the data management, data governance, and business and quality rules definitions are appropriate for the line(s) of business that they represent. Data stewards are a group of individuals each with input in the cross-enterprise data management policies and, equally importantly, with ensuring that the policies are appropriate for the business process and applications that support their line of business. Is this a full-time position for each of the data stewards? Not necessarily. In fact, since the domain expertise is such a critical factor, it is important that the data stewards maintain a fair amount of their existing responsibility so that they can continue to learn and influence business issues. So, data stewardship is an activity to which several people are committed—people that will guarantee that the best interests of their area of responsibility are reflected in the data. The people you select as data stewards should be able to work with other parts of the organization to ensure that the full scope of data provides for the needs of the entire organization. Data stewardship will take a commitment from many people across the organization.

Oddly enough, for data stewards to be truly effective, they need to be just a little more removed from the data. This might be an IT person who has a big picture view of the organization. She might not completely understand how the salesperson works on a day-in and day-out basis, but she does realize the impact that quality data can have in the salespersons activities. The data steward is not a person that has been head down in the technology. If a potential data steward talks about an IT program she wrote that slashed 10 minutes off one process, you are not talking to the right person. There is no question that there is a small pool of candidates with these qualifications, but I would not recommend that companies attempt to hire from outside for this kind of job. Unless you can find someone in a virtually identical line of business to what you are in, the business-user issues would not be addressed. Even hiring business-user savvy IT people who reached across the fence at a previous company is no guarantee that they could do the same for your organization.

Another option, then, is to hire a management consultant. But this can be tricky. You should not outsource data management initiatives as data is an organizational asset. You need to own this process. Hiring a management consultant is a form of outsourcing, but it can work if the expectations are clear. Along with having the necessary domain and IT experience, the consultant should be hands on and needs to work with your organization in identifying and training in-house data stewards.

(Continued)

This is not the kind of job where the consultant visits your company and then goes off and writes a report. The report will land on a shelf, and your data will still be a mess. Any consultant hired for this effort will only be effective if one of her primary responsibilities is the selection and training of data stewards to manage data governance deployments after the consultants are gone.

"You cannot outsource stewardship," says Peter Harvey, the CEO of Intellidyn. Although Intellidyn helps companies with their data challenges as they relate to marketing, he says it is impossible to work with a company where management isn't willing to own the data issues. "You have to have an internal champion. Otherwise, governance is just a staff exercise that never gets associated with ROI."

In the policy realm, real-time activities and preventive data quality rules and processes emerge. Organizations at this level benefit from knowing about data problems *immediately* when they occur—not a month afterwards. Data governance processes are built into the foundation of MDM, ERP, and CRM systems. Data metrics are often measured against industry standards to provide insight into areas needing improvement. The organization's data goals shift from problem correction to problem prevention. The organization moves from a data management model focused on fighting fires to one where governance is enhanced by best-in-class data management.

For technology, a data stewardship group maintains corporate data definitions and business rules. This is a standing committee that should meet regularly. The proactive organization employs data monitoring vigorously, and more real-time processing is available. Data quality functionality is shared across different operation modes. Service-oriented architecture (SOA) becomes the enterprise standard. The SOA-enabled organization is one that is transitioning from delivering applications to delivering business solutions. Application development traditionally documents the functional requirements from a vertical support point of view—the workflow is documented, procedures are defined, data objects are modeled to support those procedures, and code is written to execute those procedures within the context of the data model. The resulting product does what it needs to do and nothing more.[1]

When an organization reaches the proactive stage, corporate risks drop dramatically. Better information available throughout the enterprise increases the reliability of sound decision making. The rewards for organizations at this level increase exponentially. With a solid data quality foundation in place, proactive organizations realize better customer satisfaction and loyalty, improvements in operational efficiency and the ability to truly be an agile enterprise.

I have stressed in previous chapters the need to take data governance step by step. This may lead organizations to believe that the data improvement cycle is like an M.S. Escher stairway—it appears to lead in circles that never quite get to the destination.

The step-by-step success can be seen in the way a resort property management company began their data governance initiative. The resort operator is a leader in family destination vacations. It has properties spread around the Western Hemisphere—some built by the company and others it has acquired over time. When I first started working with this company, it housed information about guests—reservations, resort stays, and marketing information—in separate systems representing each property and maintained by each property. Not only did the company not have an accurate view of individual guests, it did not have a household view of its guests. There was no way to connect members of a household to reservations being made, nor was there any way to understand the relationship of their customers across all their properties. Although the company specializes in family vacations, it also accommodates business leisure outings and adult getaway trips. The company's goal was to create a master file and gain the real-time ability to know how and when any customer visited one of its resorts and to ensure that the systems at each of their properties was updated to reflect any customer activity at any property. And the company did not want to just combine its information, it wanted to institute data governance controls in real time. By all accounts, it was a daunting task.

To achieve this goal, all the information from all properties was combined in a central location. The various records from different properties were deduplicated, and household relationships were determined. The information was then augmented with geographic, demographic, and financial information. Finally, customer lifetime value and property effectiveness were calculated. This allowed operators taking reservations and marketers planning sales pitches to understand the true value of each household and to offer promotions specific to those households. But the consolidated master data was not limited to the execution of better campaigns—it had a far-reaching impact on all aspects of the business. In three short years, the company went from having a disjointed and incomplete view of its customer base to a unified one that has helped reduce marketing costs, offer more appropriate products, enhance property acquisition strategies, and improve the bottom line. The organization is definitely proactive and reaping the benefits.

MASTER DATA MANAGEMENT AND SERVICE-ORIENTED ARCHITECTURE'S ROLE IN DATA GOVERNANCE

One of the main objectives of a proactive organization is to support a synchronized, shared repository of information—that "single view of the truth" that I have discussed. The single version of the truth is maintained in the MDM system. There are many different technology issues associated with MDM, and these will be discussed in the final part of this book. It is important at this point to understand MDM and the value it brings to your organization. MDM, simply, is your organization reflected in your data. Data definitions and rules that have been agreed to across your organization are now reflected in your MDM system. We do not create data for the sake of data, though. We create data to improve business operations, processes, and decisions. In order to do that, we have to make sure the data is available across all operational and analytical systems. An MDM system is the mechanism by which this can happen effectively.

SOA plays a key role in helping companies achieve that vision because of its agility. As new data and information are integrated into the master data repository, proper data governance policies and procedures will ensure continuous data excellence. However, integrating and consolidating data alone will not accomplish the objectives of data governance. The true value is seen only when the consolidated master data is integrated back into operational and analytical use by the participating applications, allowing the enterprise to have a single, synchronized view of its business data. To do this, we employ a service-oriented architecture.

Tactically, a services layer must be introduced to facilitate the transition of applications to the use of a master repository. Strategically, the information in the core master entities establishes a set of information services that support the rapid and efficient development of business applications. Both of these imperatives are satisfied by SOA. In essence, there is a symbiotic relationship between data governance and SOA. SOA is centered on providing consistent services across applications. For the proactive organization, this means making sure that data is manipulated via the services layered on top of the MDM system, providing a consistent set of services. For example, there needs to be a service that will "determine if a customer is a new customer." This service should be deployed in all operational and analytic applications so that all systems run the same service. This will prevent finance or distribution from adding a new customer that already exists in a sales force automation or marketing system. The success of data governance depends on the ability to deploy and use master data and manipulation services. At the same time, a services-oriented approach to business solution development relies on the existence of a governed master data repository. Only when the consistent data services based on the master data are deployed across the enterprise will your organization truly have enterprise consistency. SOA is rapidly becoming the architectural foundation in most organizations.

THE CUSTOMER PARADOX: WHY BUSINESS RULES ARE IMPORTANT

One of the most difficult issues with advancing to the proactive stage is getting agreement across the organization. Something that should be an easy concept is not. For example, "How should we define a customer?" A basic definition of a customer might be anyone that your organization provides products or services to. Simple enough. However, different parts of the organization think differently. Marketing, for instance, will typically send "marketing products" to prospects and would consider them "customers." Their mailing and e-mail lists typically contain a lot of potential customers. Finance would consider a customer any company that pays for a good or service. Sales might typically have several contacts in an organization—and considers each of these contacts as a customer. Figure 8.1 poses the question "Who is a customer?" Is a prospect a customer? Is a customer the person who signed a contract, or is it the department within the company, or is it the company as a whole? If a customer is the person who signed the contract, what happens if she leaves the company? If a customer is the company—and the company is huge and has multiple contracts—how do you differentiate? There is no singular right answer to how to list a customer, but each company should choose a consistent way of listing customers.

> Is a customer the person who signed a contract, or is it the department within the company, or is it the company as a whole?

Once you determine what qualifies someone as a customer, you must then consider when to stop counting him as one. If sales, marketing, and

SALES

Views a customer as someone who signs a contract

MARKETING

Views a customer as someone that might buy something

FINANCE

Views a customer as someone who pays the invoice

Once that's settled, you have to decide who your customer *really* is.

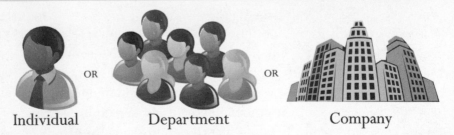

Individual   OR   Department   OR   Company

FIGURE 8.1   Who Is a Customer?

finance each have a separate file for a customer, they will each have their own rules that define when to move someone to the Inactive Customer file. Marketing still wants to send out mailings and offers, but does not want to waste money on postage and design fees when there is no hope of future business, so they want to move customers to the "Inactive Customer" file. Sales holds out hope they can turn them into repeat customers, so they might want to keep these customers as active, while finance has a rule in place that removes them from the Active Customer file after there has been no contact with the customer for a period of time. Unless there is a unified view of this customer, redundant files will show up and could affect customer relationships as well as business operations.

So, who's got the best data? One issue that data stewards need to address is which applications store the best data for which purposes. Every application, from databases that finance uses to the sales force automation tools in place, has several fields populated with data—customer name, address, phone number, e-mail, and so on. But not all fields are populated accurately or kept up to date. Along with using a tool to compare and clean files, data stewards need to select the application that is most likely to keep specific bits of data most updated and processes automated so that the entire organization has access to the generated data. For instance, which organization would you expect to maintain the most reliable and up-to-date address? A sales force automation application or the applications accounts payable uses? If you have a call center do you trust they have the most up-to-date phone numbers, or would you think distribution keeps the best data?

Comparatively speaking, addresses and phone numbers are fairly easy to make decisions about—and fix. What gets more complicated—and what proactive organizations must master—is choosing the business rules for generating data like "customer value" or "customer discount." This really speaks to the motivation of individual departments. The sales staff likes to count things like tax and shipping as part of the value of the sale because that makes the sale look higher and potentially pad their commissions or bonuses. Finance would never count the sales tax and shipping. In fact, if finance is using a solution to understand the true value of the sale, deducting the hours spent with the customer, flights to the customer's location, rounds of golf, company apparel, and dinners must be deducted as well. A similar situation emerges if the company is attempting to use marketing data to calculate the ROI of a specific campaign. Marketing might assign a high ROI value by counting only the mailing and printing costs. Finance might assign a much lower figure as it factors the man hours spent on the campaign and graphic designer bills.

All of these questions are critical to answer, but what is most important is that there needs to be one rule that every part of the organization respects. This is why executive sponsorship is integral to proactive and governed organizations. If groups within an organization cannot agree, an executive must step in to either make the call or insist that the data stewards' recommendation be followed.

Reaching the proactive stage is not easy. It requires diligence and consistency that are the responsibilities of the entire organization. More important, it requires an executive mandate and a competent set of data stewards to drive that mandate. Data is a corporate asset and is funded and treated as such. It is hard work but worth the effort. And the proactive organization has laid the foundation for a truly governed organization.

Advancing to the Next Stage

You know you have reached the proactive stage when your organization begins to unify the corporate view of a specific domain (typically customers or products). You have effectively whittled your multiple silos down to a few. The next stage creates an integrated approach for all corporate information, ultimately leading to the quality of information that can support automated business processes.

Proactive organizations trying to reach the governed stage need to think less about functions, less about data, and more about processes. Executives need to reassess the way they think about what their organization does. A pharmaceutical industry client puts it this way: "We talk about being in the business of bringing drugs to patients. We are really in the business of producing evidence and information about the safety and efficacy of drugs that we bring to patients. We're a science company, but we are supported by information management." This is the mark of a proactive organization—making information management decisions based on the need to improve the business rather than the need to improve the IT infrastructure.

To progress to the governed stage, a company needs to finish the assembly and integration of many of the pieces already in place. A Center of

Excellence or similar framework should emerge to organize the work of multiple data stewards within the enterprise. Business analysts, working through data stewards, start to control the data management process, with IT playing a supporting role. And the master data efforts provided by MDM initiatives provide a foundation for business process automation, as the data is now robust and reliable enough to support high-end process management.

The technology required to reach the final stage also centers on the ability to automate business processes. The essentials of MDM are in place, and organizations typically need to concentrate on making master data a core component, regardless of the originating application or data type. Through a high degree of data quality, the foundation for supporting full business process integration is now feasible. The ultimate goal of data quality and data governance is not really about the data at all—it is about effective, efficient, and timely business process integration. We will explore this in more detail in the next chapter.

■ NOTE

1. David Loshin, "Master Data Management and the Functional SOA Service Layer," A DataFlux "White Paper," May 2008.

CHAPTER 9

Governed Organizations: Trust in Data Pays Multiple Benefits

The first rule of any technology used in a business is that automation applied to an efficient operation will magnify the efficiency. The second rule is that automation applied to an inefficient operation will magnify the inefficiency.

—BILL GATES, FOUNDER OF MICROSOFT

EXECUTIVE OVERVIEW

Characteristics of a Governed Organization

- Think globally, act globally
- Unified data governance strategy
- Comfortable incorporating external data without fear of corrupting existing, internal data
- Executive sponsorship

Technology Adoption

- Business process automation
- Master data management (MDM)

(continued)

(Continued)

Business Capabilities

- Business requirements drive IT projects
- Repeatable, automated business processes
- Personalized customer relationships and optimized operations

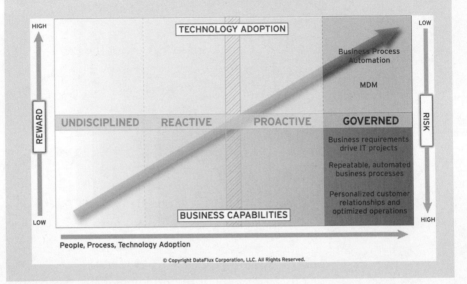

© Copyright DataFlux Corporation, LLC. All Rights Reserved.

REMEMBER

1. Data quality and data governance should *never* be considered a one-time project. A quality culture must be established as an ongoing, continuous process.

2. No organization can tackle enterprise-wide data quality and data governance all at once. To be successful, your journey must be evolutionary. Start small and take achievable steps that can be measured along the way.

Governed organizations trust their data. They trust that they can make strategic decisions based on it. They trust that they can automate processes that are dependent on the data. In a world where compliance issues can sink an organization, where investor trust is often lacking, it is critical to know that your data is sound. In governed organizations there is not "a cottage industry of extra activity built around trying to figure out if the data is right" according to Mike Ferguson, a globally recognized consultant on data management issues and president of Intelligent Business Strategies.

The governed organization has a unified data governance strategy throughout the enterprise. Data quality, data integration, and data synchronization are integral parts of all business processes, and the organization achieves impressive results from a single, unified view of the enterprise. It is a "think globally, act globally" mindset that is driven by a desire to have data standards managed as rigorously as the financial assets.

Governed organizations pay attention to the subjective aspects of data quality such as believability, relevance, and trust factors. These factors are looked at alongside more traditional metrics such as completeness, correctness, and duplication. The governed organization is comfortable incorporating third-party data on aspects like credit, demographics, and sociographic levels, without the fear that this outside data will clash with, or corrupt, existing data. Governed organizations know that complex quality initiatives are needed to support a business management strategy. They seek to identify and remove the causes of defects and errors in business processes using quality management methodologies like Six Sigma. They know they are more likely to succeed because the data to support the processes is accurate.

PROFILE OF A GOVERNED ORGANIZATION

The key benefit of being a governed organization is having sufficient faith in your data to automate many business processes, freeing up valuable resources to work on other strategic initiatives. Business processes, such as selecting which goods to send to stores, ordering parts, order-to-cash, and creating e-mail marketing lists, can all be done with fewer personnel resources and better results.

A company that achieves this stage can focus on providing superior customer service, as they grow to understand various facets of a customer's interactions. This is possible due to a single repository of all relevant information and a consistent set of data services that are available to the various applications based on the master data.

Combining disparate data silos is critical to reaching this stage. All data is managed at the same level, available to business users throughout the organization. Many proactive organizations reach the point where they have good, very clean, useable, and comprehensive data on the sales and marketing side and equally clean, useable, and comprehensive data on the production side. But the sides do not talk to each other—with the exception of, perhaps, a few forecast tools that struggle to pull data from one side and use it to help the other. So the organization might be able to automate marketing messages and supply chain issues, but it cannot go beyond that to tailor marketing messages to issues occurring in production and vice versa.

Let's look at the value of governed data to food producers that market their own products. Historical data and forecasting tools have helped these companies select the right specials or coupons. The explosion of shopper cards and automated systems for gathering customer data have dramatically improved the ability of organizations in this sector to target offers to different shopper segments in order to encourage repeat business while maximizing revenue and profit. An example is the targeted coupons that are printed out at the time a shopper checks out, promoting products the customer already buys or could be convinced to buy.

Given the disconnected nature of most data sources, I would venture that more than a few food producers have been burned when a commodity spike occurred at the same time a coupon went out for a product featuring that commodity. Clean, linked data can help companies create offers that reflect what is happening from the earliest stages of the supply chain, not just at the point of sale.

THE IMPORTANT PEOPLE OF DATA GOVERNANCE

What other characteristics are important for the governed organization? From the perspective of its people, data governance has executive-level sponsorship with direct CEO support. The CEO understands data, its value, and the necessity of giving it priority treatment. I have quoted Peter Harvey, CEO of Intellidyn, in earlier chapters because he has a knack for summing up the critical importance of data to the organization. When it comes to executive-level sponsorship he draws an analogy to Moses getting the Ten Commandments. Only, in this case the CEO is the corporate god that "has to tell everyone this is what we are going to do," Harvey says.

Business users take an active role in data strategy and delivery. In a governed organization, people would never consider keeping their own spreadsheets of data because they do not trust the organization's data. Nor are these business users building their own silos of information or, conversely, begging for information from IT. Those days are long gone. Instead, a data quality or data governance group works directly with data stewards, application developers, and database administrators. Everyone is on the same page. The organization has zero defects policies for data collection and management. "Zero defects" is not a slogan—it becomes reality.

Do individuals at governed organizations ever disagree about how to manage data? Of course. But unlike their less-governed brethren, the issues are dealt with quickly and proactively with the involvement of engaged, knowledgeable executives. New initiatives, for instance, are only approved after careful consideration of how the initiatives will impact the existing data infrastructure. Automated policies are in place to ensure that data remains consistent, accurate, and reliable throughout the enterprise. And as we discussed in Chapter 8, these automated processes are integrated to the data via service-oriented architecture (SOA) which encapsulates business rules for quality data.

In order to achieve this level, it is critical that data quality and data integration tools be standardized across the organization. It is also critical that all aspects of the organization use standard business rules created and maintained by data stewards. A sale is assigned the same dollar value (and only assigned to the system once) whether sales, marketing, finance, or production is capturing it.

In the governed organization, data is continuously inspected, and any deviations from standards are resolved immediately. While governed organizations may use an outside company to help with some aspects of data maintenance and governance, the governed organization does not permanently outsource data issues. Instead, they own this process. Data models capture the business meaning and technical details of all corporate data elements.

The discussion of the governed organization is probably not complete without a little discussion on data models. Remember, we are trying to provide consistency in data across your entire organization. The data consistency is reflected in your enterprise data model—the model that de-fines the data in the best representation of the stakeholders, business users, and data stewards. A consistent, universally accepted data model is the most difficult aspect for the governed organization to achieve. The model has to reflect the best data from across the organization, and there has to be agree-ment from all aspects of the organization that it is indeed the best represen-tation. What does this mean? People from different lines of business with different responsibilities have to agree on the most basic aspects of your company. Very basic questions have to be answered. Questions like who is a customer? Does a prospect belong in your customer database? Is a sales contact a customer, or is the company they work for a customer? Is a cus-tomer a customer if it has received your products but never paid your in-voice? The questions get more difficult and more complicated as you proceed down the company. This is why "people" is the most difficult and important aspect of the governed organization.

What Does a Governed Organization Look Like?

For governed organizations, risks are low, and reward is high. Master data is so tightly controlled across the enterprise that the organization can maintain high-quality information about its customers, prospects, inventory, and pro-ducts. The rewards are numerous. Corporate data practices can lead to a bet-ter understanding about an organization's current business landscape, allowing management to have full confidence in data-based decisions.

At this stage of the maturity model, a major culture shift has occurred within the entire organization. Instead of treating issues of data quality and data integration as a series of tactical projects, these companies have a com-prehensive program that elevates the process of managing business-critical data. With support from executive management and buy-in from all busi-ness functions, the program can flourish, creating more consistent, accu-rate, and reliable information to support the entire organization.

More important, the company can automate processes that once re-quired necessary and time-consuming human intervention. Business pro-cess automation becomes a reality, and enterprise systems can work to meet the needs of employees, not vice versa.

WHAT'S NEXT?

Do you want to have full confidence in data-based decisions? Do you want to automate laborious business processes? Do you want the revenue, profit, and reputational benefits that accrue for organizations that have their data house in order? If you have answered "yes" to these questions, then keep reading, and I will give you some more specifics on how to do this.

In Part Three we will take an in-depth look at the people and processes needed to grow into a governed organization. I will get into a little more detail about the importance of executive input and how you likely already have all the people you need to reach governed status on your staff right now. With people, it is often a matter of helping them find the right roles and organizing them in a way that promotes cross–business-unit coordination. For processes, I will introduce you to a life-cycle that is simple to implement and is repeatable—think of it as a staircase that helps you wind your way to the top of the hill. You may feel out of breath at times, but it beats the alternative: sitting at the base of the hill watching others climb it.

PART THREE

Utilizing People and Processes to Achieve a Quality Culture

CHAPTER 10

The Quality Culture

Quality is not an act, it is a habit.

ARISTOTLE

EXECUTIVE OVERVIEW

Before reading another page in this book, it is important that you buy into the idea that you have the power to move your company into the governed stage. Even if you are looking at your organization, shaking your head and asking, *How on Earth will I do this?* The fact that you are looking shows the potential for growth.

Here is what we have learned so far:

- Data is entering our organizations at an ever-increasing rate.
- Data has the potential to make our businesses successful, or it can lead to disaster.

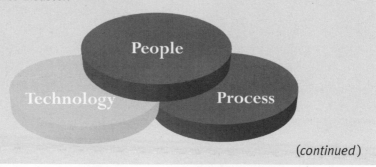

(continued)

(Continued)
- Data should be treated and funded as a corporate asset.
- Sound data management practices require constant and long-term attention.

Given the important role data can play in organizations, it is critical to approach data management with sound, repeatable processes and to create a culture of quality for all data initiatives.

Part Two gave you the information needed to assess your organization's location on the Data Governance Maturity Model and a framework for becoming a more mature organization. In this part, I will take an in-depth look at the people and process requirements (technology requirements will be discussed in Part Four) for creating a quality culture—a culture that will put you on the path to becoming a governed organization. You will see how making a few key business process adjustments, coupled with empowering capable people and providing the right technology, will pay almost immediate dividends. You will learn how to develop a quality culture and how to execute effectively.

Remember

1. Data quality and data governance should *never* be considered a one-time project. A quality culture must be established as an ongoing, continuous process.

2. No organization can tackle enterprise-wide data quality and data governance all at once. To be successful, your journey must be evolutionary. Start small and take achievable steps that can be measured along the way.

Since Aristotle first created the classification concept 23 centuries ago, we've thought of information as something that is gathered, indexed and—with the advent of computers—stored. All of these verbs make us think of inanimate objects. Makes sense, right? Data, after all, isn't a living thing.

Although data is not a living being, it certainly takes on a life of its own. With that in mind, I believe that you don't gather, store or index data—you govern it. You coordinate the people, process, and technology needed to enable an organization to leverage information as a corporate asset. Data becomes another asset like your workforce, your production machinery or your facilities. You have policies that govern each of these items. Now you need to govern your data to keep it effective and useful.

In Aristotle's effort to classify all the knowledge around him he truly discovered that the whole really is more than the sum of its parts. Aristotle also had something else to say that makes great sense when it comes to the data companies need to govern: Quality is not an act, it is a habit. Let's learn the good habits of data quality to improve our corporate operations and decision making. The end result is that better data makes for better operations. Better data makes for better decision making. Better data makes for better business.

QUALITY AND DATA: MORE THAN JUST GETTING THE NUMBERS RIGHT

I was in New York City recently, waiting to cross the street, and the importance of quality was manifest to me. As yellow cabs were zooming by, I was impressed by something we take for granted every day—the relationship between the crosswalk lights, the stop lights, and the pedestrians. People were waiting at the street corner, their eyes glued to the glowing red hand on the other side of the street, warning them it was not safe to cross. When the stoplight changed from green to red, the red hand disappeared and gave way to a white stick figure depicting a person walking (see Figure 10.1).

FIGURE 10.1   Street Crossing Signal

As if a whistle had been blown, all of the pedestrians started crossing the street without even as much as a glance at the oncoming traffic. In this case, a quality deficiency in the symmetry between the stop lights and the crosswalk lights could have been fatal. The people waiting on the sidewalk had total confidence in the quality and timing between the two sets of lights.

Just like those New Yorkers, you should expect the same level of quality from the data within your organization. Data systems and sources must interact and share information in order to successfully support your business objectives. And there is nothing pedestrian about that.

The requirements for methodical quality practices are all around us. While in New York, I thought about how bridges and a passing city bus depend on quality to stay intact and deliver passengers successfully.

When John Roebling designed the Brooklyn Bridge (Figure 10.2) in the late 1800s, he made it six times as strong as he thought it needed to be. However, in 1878, as the steel strand cables that would help support the bridge were being wound, inferior wire was discovered. A contractor, J. Lloyd Haigh, had been knowingly providing substandard wire to the building site. Roebling's son, Washington, proceeded with construction

FIGURE 10.2   **Brooklyn Bridge**

after determining the fallible wire would still leave the bridge four times as strong as it needed to be. While this architectural marvel still stands today, it is easy to imagine the results if the bridge had not been designed with some wiggle room for quality failures. Now look at your organization. Is it built to withstand bad data, or would a project on which you are working collapse?

Establishing a quality culture will ensure that you are using the highest-quality materials which will support your organization for years to come.

Another example of something that relies heavily on quality is the city bus. Just think of all the moving parts in the bus that must function in order for the bus to accelerate, turn, and stop. Everything from the left turn signal to the seat spacing for passengers is important for a quality trip from Point A to Point B. The tires must be able to survive potholes, rocks, curbs, and anything else in its path. If the buses continually break down, the passengers will quit using them.

If you have disparate systems that are not communicating with each other, it is the same as having shoddy equipment on the bus. Your bad data could cause customers to abandon their efforts—and this could lead to disjointed decision making within your organization.

Your organization's data has the same needs as a crosswalk signal, a bridge or a bus when it comes to quality. Your organization requires quality at all stages—when data enters the database, when it interacts with other data sources, and when it is extracted for business usage. Without quality data, projects will fail, and confusion will reign.

WHAT IS THE QUALITY CULTURE?

At this point in the book you are probably wondering why someone did not try earlier to steer your organization in a better direction. Until recently, companies have not been encouraged to look at their data at the enterprise-wide level. Instead, the focus was on getting a quick fix with maximum return on investment (ROI). The emphasis has been on localized projects instead of corporatewide execution. Business units brought problems to the IT team. The IT team was supposed to build specific applications to solve each specific problem. Despite the obvious difficulties that have arisen from this strategy, the results have not been all bad. After all, the lessons learned from the efforts to consolidate data from disparate systems placed a spotlight on the need for a more deliberate approach that values sound data practices that provide a solid infrastructure and repeatable processes.

Rapid changes in the marketplace have further driven home this new mandate. These changes include:

- Increased compliance regulations and risk assessments that force organizations to look at the enterprise as a whole, compiling and viewing their organizations as more than just their individual components.

- An economic downturn that requires organizations to do more with less and to refocus on better management practices instead of isolated projects.

- Competitive pressures that drive organizations to take advantage of one of the few proprietary assets they have—their data.

Each of these changes is reflected in behaviors linked to an organization's culture of quality. Organizations use several methods to examine quality. Manufacturers have quality standards to ensure there are methodologies in place for each part of the company. A company's books are audited by a third party. Even Microsoft Word users have a quality tool to check their work—in the form of spell check.

To establish a quality culture, you do not need an out-of-the-box quality methodology, and you cannot rely on periodic data quality audits. Rather, you need to create a mindset of quality throughout the organization with team members dedicated to maintaining the integrity of data across the enterprise with processes and technology to back up the effort.

WHY QUALITY SHOULD BE FORWARD-THINKING

British anthropologist/philosopher Gregory Bateson used to tell a story about replacing the beams in one of the dining halls at Oxford University. While the story is a good bit of fiction, it is a great story. The anecdote goes something like this:

On the grounds of New College, Oxford, about 100 years ago, an entomologist climbed into the rafters of the dining hall, stuck a pen knife into the large oak beams supporting the ceiling and found a beetle infestation. When the College's administration learned of the problem they immediately began to wonder where they would be able to find such large and high quality beams.

As the tale goes, the college's forester told the administration that since oak beams often get infested with beetles the college had the foresight 500 years ago to plant a grove of oak trees to replace the beams in question. And better yet, each forester told the incoming forester about the grove and what those trees would eventually be used for—in case there was ever a temptation to cut them down for some other reason.

We may not be working with wood beams and 500-year timelines, but the message to plan ahead comes through clearly. An organization with a quality culture understands this, so it establishes a solid infrastructure and repeatable processes. New data is seamlessly integrated into existing systems or when bad data is identified, it is cleaned and incorporated. These processes also ensure data is shared across different platforms and systems, so that business users are all looking at—and making decisions from—the same information.

We also need to talk about what a quality culture eschews—a fixation on rapid ROI at the expense of long-term success. And since we are using tree analogies, let's talk about another one. I live in a neighborhood with lots of beautiful old trees. After a recent hurricane, those trees were still standing. The recently planted ornamental pear trees, however, were split down the middle—their heavy limbs dangling off of cars and mailboxes. Horticulturists have known for a while that this particular variety of ornamental pear is prone to wind and ice damage at about the 15-year point. But homeowners and developers continue to plant them, and the reason is simple: They grow extremely fast and, when in bloom, they're gorgeous. For developers that want an instant streetscape, ornamental pears offer a quick route.

With data, organizations are also looking for superfast solutions and quick fixes—perhaps figuring the problem with that approach can be off-loaded to someone down the line. Ultimately, that just leaves organizations more vulnerable to long-term problems.

The quality culture provides you with the tools and knowledge to get back to the basics. It emphasizes fundamentals over rapid development; it stresses repeatability over one-off projects. And, the quality culture provides your organization with solid practices and infrastructure that will make any future project more successful and more integrated with the rest of your organization. Unless you establish a quality culture and are forward-thinking, each time a new project is started, you will have to start back at square one.

QUALITY CULTURE: ROADMAP TO DATA GOVERNANCE

Understanding the importance and need for a quality culture is critical to your success in establishing data governance. However, it is not something that can be developed with just technology. It is a combination of shifting the way people in your organization think, redefining the processes and then securing the technology to implement the changes. You have likely heard technology vendors tell you "Success requires emphasis on people, process, and technology." And in the next breath, they will say "Let me tell you about my technology." Well, let me take some time to talk to you about the people and processes, because as far as I'm concerned, technology may be the most straightforward of the three to implement.

CHAPTER 11

People

The number one benefit of information technology is that it empowers people to do what they want to do. It lets people be creative. It lets people be productive. It lets people learn things they didn't think they could learn before, and so in a sense it is all about potential.

—STEVE BALLMER, MICROSOFT CEO

EXECUTIVE OVERVIEW

Achieving a quality culture starts with people. Building the right team that can support the business goals by utilizing sound processes and technology is critical to achieving success. This chapter will cover several key roles and needs that you must fill in order to advance your company along the Data Governance Maturity Model.

- **The importance of executive involvement.** Employees will not respond to a quality initiative unless executives ensure they are measured on their participation and cooperation. Executives also possess the budget control necessary to create and maintain data quality and data governance initiatives.

- **The need to create buy-in from employees across the organization.** Everyone, from call-center employees to sales representatives,

(continued)

129

(Continued)

needs to understand the value of data and their role in keeping it fit for use.

- **The critical role of data stewards.** These individuals are the Renaissance Men and Women of your organization. They understand the business users' needs and the IT staff concerns, and they form the bridge linking the two parts of the organization in a constructive way.
- **The role of stakeholders, business experts, and IT.** Stakeholders and business experts should create the rules that govern the data. They can answer the "what" and "why" of data gathering. IT needs to focus on execution.

While you read this chapter, keep these key takeaways in mind as you begin to formulate your people plan:

- IT needs to do what IT does best: manage the deployment, administration, and maintenance of data and applications.
- Business users must drive the data and applications so that IT is not viewed as a cost center, but rather as a critical player in the business's success.
- Each side needs to understand and value the role of data stewards.

Remember

1. Data quality and data governance should *never* be considered a one-time project. A quality culture must be established as an ongoing, continuous process.

2. No organization can tackle enterprise-wide data quality and data governance all at once. To be successful, your journey must be evolutionary. Start small and take achievable steps that can be measured along the way.

There is an old Chinese proverb that can serve as a fundamental theme for helping the people in your organization adjust to a quality culture. The proverb says:

Tell me and I'll forget; show me and I may remember; involve me and I'll understand.

The quality culture requires people to change the way they approach their jobs, interact with their peers, and prioritize their work. People do not like to change. They will toss up roadblocks, voice excuses, and plot resistance. The best way to thwart these efforts is to get them involved. Throughout this book I have stressed the need for cooperation and collaboration—across the IT/ business barrier and across lines of business. I have also stressed the importance of executive sponsorship and support. Both of these deserve a closer look.

EXECUTIVE SPONSORSHIP

The quality culture will impact all aspects of your organization. Everyone will not be impacted at once, but they will all eventually experience changes in the processes they follow and the functions they perform. Maybe that sounds a bit melodramatic, or perhaps you have trouble seeing how implementing a quality culture for data management can have such a far-reaching impact. Consider some of the changes that you may experience:

- Call-center staff will be asked to change the way they acquire information from customers, the way they navigate their call-center applications, and the way they input data into the system.
- Sales people will need to concentrate on consistency of customer, product, and sales information.
- Accounts payable will have different processes to determine if they are invoicing existing customers and will need to choose from a consistent set of product deliverables.
- Even the manufacturing production line will be asked to change the way they organize and inventory parts and raw materials.

Certainly, not all processes and not all people will be affected immediately, and not all people will be affected to the same degree. But, over time, as quality becomes a consistent mantra, people will need to embrace the change.

In order to get effective participation across all aspects of your business, the initiative must be supported from the top. Executive management must provide the direction and delegate the authority for these activities to be successful. In addition, any change that is going to impact different aspects of your organization is going to require collaboration. There needs to be

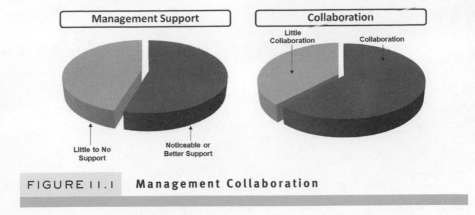

FIGURE 11.1   **Management Collaboration**

consensus across departments, lines of business, and applications. Gaining this consensus requires executive support. BARC, a technology consulting and analyst firm in Germany, recently published a survey that, among other questions, asked organizations about the amount of collaboration that was evident in their organization. In addition, they asked how much executive sponsorship was experienced. Figure 11.1 shows the correlation between executive sponsorship and collaboration.

You can clearly see a direct correlation between the amount of executive support and the amount of collaboration that occurs in an organization. The way to get management support is to ensure that the justification for the quality culture is firmly rooted in initiatives that add business value.

THE RIGHT TEAM

For years, we have been faced with a conundrum: IT manages technology it does not use and business units often use technology they do not control. And, for years, we have been unhappy with this gulf. Business users are quick to point out that the applications that come from IT are insufficient for their business needs. IT is quick to point out that business does not properly articulate needs and changes their minds too often. It is a constant battle of finger pointing and buck passing.

Where has this left us? On the one hand, you have business users that cannot optimally perform their jobs. On the other hand, the IT staff grows frustrated with their contribution and with their roles. This leads to a business that is not functioning productively and will ultimately not be competitive.

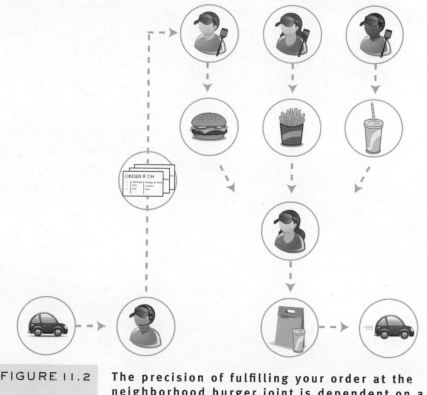

FIGURE 11.2   **The precision of fulfilling your order at the neighborhood burger joint is dependent on a well-rehearsed process and people being trained and executing that training**

This scenario is not just seen in office settings. Think of your local hamburger joint (see Figure 11.2). When you walk in and place your order, there are several things going on behind the scenes. Let's say you order a hamburger, french fries, and a drink, to go. Each person behind the counter may have their own idea of how to please you as a customer. The person taking your order wants to collect the right amount of money and make the correct change. The person putting food in your bag needs to make sure all the items are in there. The person in the back is cooking your hamburger and paying attention to any requested deviations (no pickle, extra ketchup, and so on). The restaurant manager is concerned with all of these things, but most of all, wants you to have a good experience so you will come back again and again.

Now, think about what would happen if the order taker did not enter your order correctly. His coworkers would not be able to accomplish their jobs. What if no one trains the bag packer to carefully put a lid on the drink cup? That certainly will negatively affect your experience. And if you take that first bite into your lunch, as you are driving down the road, and you realize you do not have what you ordered because the cook in the back made an error, you may think twice about going back to the restaurant.

The best restaurants have established processes that trained staff are expected to follow. Each time an order is placed, it initiates a series of steps that gets your food cooked, packaged, and delivered in the most efficient manner possible. The best processes, however, will not work if the people performing them do not carry them out correctly.

It is the same for your business and your data. Even with the most robust and advanced processes, you are doomed to fail if your people are not on board, supportive, and capable. So, how can you go about achieving that?

The key is to let IT enable the business instead of focusing exclusively on enabling technologies. Through an installation of new software or a deployment of an innovative tool, most organizations find their IT department dealing with technology. However, empowering IT to enable business is a key step in adopting a quality culture. This enablement begins when company executives support the quality culture and stress its importance. It continues when IT understands what business users are trying to accomplish, what information they need, and how it is being used. The traditional comfort zone of just managing technology for the sake of technology is gone. In today's Information Age, IT has to align its goals with those of business users.

So, how does IT become an enabler of business? In every organization, applications will come and go—proprietary systems will give way to packaged applications, and packaged applications will be consolidated to larger packaged applications. Changes in technology or changes in your business will drive you to further application deployments. People also come and go in every organization. Whether they move to another role in the company or leave for opportunities elsewhere, the knowledge about systems and processes often goes with them. Twenty-five percent of all employees have been with their organization for less than a year. Fifty percent of all employees have been at their organization for less than five years.[1] People come and people go. Applications are deployed and retired. Businesses evolve. Regardless of the personnel, application infrastructure or business changes going on around you—there is one thing that will survive all changes and all corporate evolution. And, that one thing is your data.

To evolve into a quality culture, you must build a team that is going to promote an active alliance between the business and IT, and a consistent data environment that will survive the inevitable changes in your organization.

In Part Two, the roles of many of the people that are critical to creating a quality culture were defined—executives, stakeholders, business analysts, data stewards, and IT professionals. The list is long, and each role has its own measure of success. So, how do we get all of these folks to get along and operate as a team? By defining a structure that promotes cooperation. Your data team should be organized so that IT maintains the information technology environment for best practices in data management. Business professionals can then manage the definition of data for best practices in business. Figure 11.3 shows how the overall structure should look.

What are the important aspects of this organization?

- Business users must drive the data and applications requirements.
- IT focuses on managing the deployment, administration, and main-tenance of data and applications.
- Data stewards provide the glue between business and IT.

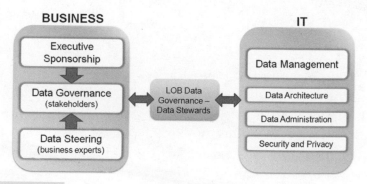

FIGURE 11.3   **Data stewards bridge the gap between business and IT**

By now, I think you understand the structure of what a quality culture looks like. Now you are probably wondering, *How does it work?* To answer this, we need a more in-depth discussion about the role of the people involved in the quality culture.

A Look at the Key Players

I have discussed the players that need to be involved in a successful data governance program at a very high level. Now, let's take a closer look at the way to structure your organization for successful management of data. Looking at the various roles in the business/IT relationship diagram (Figure 11.3), we need to take a closer look at executives, stakeholders, business executives, IT professionals, and, perhaps the most critical role in the quality culture, data stewards.

What are the responsibilities of these roles? More importantly, how do they interact with each other to ensure success?

Executive Sponsors: Improvement Starts at the Top

Senior management support is critical to an enterprise-wide activity like data governance. Executives have budget authority and revenue goals. As executives prioritize engagements by the rest of the organization, their support keeps data governance on the front burner. Executives are best able to communicate a strategic view to oversee and communicate the long-term value of data governance initiatives.

Executives have the ability to promote collaboration by making it an objective by which employees are measured. Executives also have budgetary control, something that is critical to ensuring adequate funding of data quality and governance initiatives. An executive is in the best position to select appropriate people and vest them with the authority necessary to get the job done. It is pretty simple really. If the boss considers it a priority, the staff will, too.

Of course, to get the support of senior management, you have to make the business case for data governance. Executives are concerned about how to generate revenue, cut costs, and reduce risk. Keep these key business drivers in mind when building the business case for data governance.

STAKEHOLDERS: WHERE THE RUBBER MEETS THE ROAD

Stakeholders are the business owners of data. They are the people that manage lines of business and functional areas. A stakeholder could be the marketing director that is trying to segment customers based on household value. It could be a forecaster who is trying to determine how much holiday stock to order for each store. It could be the head of procurement that is responsible for getting the right supplies to the right facility just in time. The success of the stakeholders is in the quality of the data that they rely upon to make decisions.

These stakeholders are often quite attached to their own data silos and need to be convinced that enterprise-wide data is a positive thing. Stakeholders must respect the need to consolidate and cleanse data and not be tempted to gather and store data selectively outside the company's data governance system.

Stakeholders cannot be successful unless executives have given them the *responsibility* and *authority* to ensure that data governance processes are effectively executed. Stakeholders, with their position of authority, must publicize the responsibility—as well as the penalties for noncompliance. Stakeholders are usually closely aligned with the business experts and data stewards to make sure that decisions about data governance meet the requirements of the line of business.

BUSINESS EXPERTS: STEERING FOR SUCCESS

Every department or line of business has a small handful of people that are always consulted for their expertise and knowledge. They know how things work within their line of business and they know how to make things better. The stakeholders are usually very dependent on the business experts for advice as well as execution. Business experts have a thorough understanding of all aspects of the business that are within their domain. They understand the business processes and the decisions and rules that dictate the way their functional areas operate.

The business experts play a pivotal role by using their expertise to steer the data governance committee. They are critical in crafting the appropriate data definitions and rules. They ensure that the data models, the data rules, and the data usage are fit for the needs of their line of business. The business experts will work closely with the data stewards to ensure decisions are made that satisfy both their understanding of the business and the technical requirements of the applications and technologies. The business domain experts need to understand what kind of data stakeholders need and how they use it. As subject matter experts, they also participate in the business process modeling and data requirements analysis process. The stakeholders are going to rely on the business experts to steer the data governance processes appropriately for their line of business.

Data Stewards: The Renaissance Men and Women of Your Organization

While it may seem that the person you identify as a data steward in your organization needs to be able to bend steel and repel bullets like Superman, the truth is they need to be more like a modern-day Leonardo da Vinci. Only instead of painting and inventing, she is comfortable with technology and business problems. With those broad skills comes the ability to focus laser-like attention on the data.

To find a qualified candidate to fill this role, you need to look for characteristics that will make them (and your business) successful. Because data stewards play such a critical role in the collaboration between business and IT, they must be able to speak the language of both groups and know what it all means. Think of someone with a CB radio driving down the interstate, trying to talk with truck drivers. Unless they know what "Watch out for the alligator just after the chicken coop at marker two-two-zero" means, no one is going to listen to them.

Exactly what role is the data steward playing? In an effort to achieve cross-enterprise consistency, organizations have to make decisions about how the data best represents the organization. As these decisions are made, the data steward plays the crucial role of:

1. Representing the best interests of the line of business stakeholder to ensure that data decisions that are made are compatible with the stakeholder needs.

2. Representing the IT experts to ensure that the decisions that are made can be implemented and supported by the technology that supports the functional area.

Hopefully, you can see why the data steward is the glue that holds things together, supporting the interests of the business and IT and ensuring that data decisions will meet the needs of both.

Data stewards are typically empowered to represent a line of business. As data decisions are made for all lines of business, it is the data stewards' job to speak up when a decision will not work for their specific line of business—and actively seek a solution that works for everyone. A successful data steward will have a background in business with in-depth IT knowledge, or the data steward will be a technology person who possesses business savvy and understands your business. It is also important to find someone with a problem-solving personality. Diplomatic skills do not hurt either. In any event, do not settle for less. Data stewards are the catalysts that help business and IT, as well as multiple lines of business, operate in good faith.

IT Experts: Making It All Work

IT experts are the application owners, information architects, and system analysts that keep the data flowing through the company. They understand the applications and underlying IT structure, and they need to make sure operational requirements are documented and incorporated into the quality process. Fundamentally, data governance must accommodate the current needs of the existing applications while supporting the requirements for future business changes. In turn, the system analysts must begin to reframe how they understand the way that data governance impacts different applications and to develop the services that interact with the core master architecture from the point of view of the business application and its associated clients.

Working closely with the data stewards, the IT experts will help integrate the decisions made by business into the IT architecture that runs the business. Oftentimes, there will be conflict between the needs of the business and the capabilities of the applications and IT infrastructure. This is why it is so important for the IT experts and the data stewards to work together. Using the data stewards as their voice back to the business, IT can assess the appropriateness of the data governance decisions at the most technical level and recommend alternatives in the event that there is conflict.

The IT experts have many responsibilities:

- Integration of the business requirements into IT systems
- Building and maintaining an IT architecture that supports the business
- Ensuring that IT infrastructure meets the service requirements of the business in terms of access, response time, and availability
- Implementation of policies for privacy and security of the applications and databases

One final point about personnel and the pursuit of the quality culture. You may not currently have the expertise in house. Or you may have the expertise but may not be sure how to identify it. If this is true, do not worry—most organizations have the same struggle. Many sources of expertise exist to help you find the right people to fill critical data governance roles, to help you identify data stewards, and to help you manage the relationship between business and IT. And, you do not have to do it alone. This is one area where spending a little money to bring in an experienced professional consultant or an industry thought leader can pay substantial dividends to your organization. If you need it, get professional consulting help.

■ NOTE

1. Karl Fisch and Scott McLeod, "Shift Happens, Globalization and the Information Age." June 22, 2007. YouTube Video.

CHAPTER 12

Processes

Virtually every company will be going out and empowering their workers with a certain set of tools, and the big difference in how much value is received from that will be how much the company steps back and really thinks through their business processes . . . thinking through how their business can change, how their project management, their customer feedback, their planning cycles can be quite different than they ever were before.

—BILL GATES, MICROSOFT CHAIRMAN AND FOUNDER

EXECUTIVE OVERVIEW

Motivating your staff to agree to and sign off on a process for managing data is critical to achieving a quality culture. A multiple-step lifecycle can provide a manageable, repeatable approach that companies can easily adopt. The lifecycle approach also need not be done on every bit of data the company has all at once. It can be executed in phases. In this chapter you will learn how to:

- **Discover** the importance of documenting the data in your organization and the characteristics of that data. Data discovery arms you with information about the accuracy, consistency, and reliability of your data.

- **Design** a single data model, a single set of business rules, and a single set of business processes.

(Continued)

(Continued)

- **Enable** universally agreed upon requirements that can be validated and deployed.
- **Maintain** the data with constant vigilance and continuous care. This is not a "do it once and you're done" process.
- **Archive** data that is no longer of use to your organization or update data that needs to evolve as your business evolves.

Remember

1. Data quality and data governance should *never* be considered a one-time project. A quality culture must be established as an ongoing, continuous process.

2. No organization can tackle enterprise-wide data quality and data governance all at once. To be successful, your journey must be evolutionary. Start small and take achievable steps that can be measured along the way.

W hen I pour a tall glass of cold milk, I do not think about the processes the milk went through to get to my refrigerator. I just know that if the expiration date has not passed on the carton, I can count on it being safe and tasty. There are lots of things we take for granted. But if it were not for processes that were carefully thought out and fol-

> life • cy • cle
> [lahyf-/sahy-kuh l]
> noun. The various stages through which an organism passes.

lowed, I could confidently pour myself a glass of milk and drink it without concerns of bacteria making me sick.

One hundred and fifty years ago, you needed to have access to a cow to ensure a steady supply of milk. When milk began to make its way off of farms and into cities in the early part of the twentieth century, it was not uncommon for it to be contaminated or just plain dangerous. Raw milk has living organisms that cause it to spoil pretty quickly. And if a cow is sick, drinking milk that has not been treated can cause severe illness. In 1938, milk products were the source of 25 percent of all traceable food and waterborne illnesses.[1]

The process of pasteurization changed all that. Over time, scientists determined the right temperature to heat milk and the right temperature to

store it after pasteurization. Pasteurization processes and standards have evolved to make milk much safer. Today, milk products account for less than one percent of all food and waterborne illnesses.

So what does data have to do with pasteurization? Many organizations are still in the early twentieth century when it comes to data processes. It is not managed in a consistent way, and I would venture to say it is making some of our organizations ill.

We must manage our data in the same fashion that we manage any process—with a defined, predictable methodology. This requires a data management lifecycle methodology that helps us understand how to manage, monitor, and maintain our data to benefit our business. In this chapter, I will look in detail at the lifecycle methodology (see Figure 12.1)—a methodology to be repeated any time new data enters your organization.

The data management lifecycle has five steps:

Step 1: Discover

Step 2: Design

Step 3: Enable

Step 4: Maintain

Step 5: Archive

| FIGURE 12.1 | **Lifecycle Management** |

It is difficult to separate the process from the people and technologies used to carry out the process. But to keep from getting overwhelmed, I am going to concentrate on the activities and technologies at each step in the process and the role people play in each phase.

DISCOVER

 One of the biggest mistakes that most organizations make is that they do not properly understand their data. A quick inspection of your data would probably find that it resides in many different databases, managed by many different systems, with many different formats and representations of the same data. Data can be useful only if you understand where it is, what it means to your organization, and how it relates to other data in your organization. Discovery allows you to understand just that.

> "Where shall I begin, please your Majesty?"
> "Begin at the beginning," the King said gravely.
> —Lewis Carroll, *Alice's Adventures in Wonderland*

It might strike you as odd to discuss data discovery by quoting from *Alice's Adventures in Wonderland*. The truth is, though, that many organizations find that their data is as confusing to them as Wonderland was to Alice. Can the following quotes that describe Alice's adventures also be used to describe how you feel about your organization's data?

> "I don't believe there's an atom of meaning in it."

> "This is very important." "Unimportant, of course, I meant—important, unimportant, unimportant, important."

"I think you might do something better with your time than waste it asking riddles that have no answers."

"Curiouser and curiouser."

Alice faced a blitz of unintelligible answers and nonsensical conclusions. This problem is all too common in organizations today. Many times, organizations do not make the best decision because they cannot access the right data. Many times, a decision is made based on data that is faulty or untrustworthy. However confusing the situation in Wonderland, or however confusing the data in your organization, the king in Alice's *Adventures in Wonderland* had the right idea: "Begin at the beginning."

Data discovery is essentially about the beginning. It is a fundamental, but often overlooked, step that should begin every initiative that involves data. Every enterprise resource planning (ERP) implementation, every customer relationship management (CRM) deployment, every data warehouse development, every data migration or consolidation initiative, and every application rewrite should start with data discovery. Every time you need to integrate or consolidate data sources or any time that new data sources enter your organization, start with data discovery.

Estimates for ERP and data warehouse implementation failures or severe cost overruns often run as high as 65 to 75 percent. In almost every instance, the failures, large cost overruns, and long implementation cycles are due to the same problem—a fundamental misunderstanding about the quality, meaning, or completeness of the data that is essential to the initiative. These are problems that should be identified and corrected prior to beginning the project. Data discovery is the set of activities that identify data, determine its role in the organization, and uncover problems, inconsistencies, inaccuracies, and generally unreliable data.

Data discovery has several components to it, and each prepares you for your data initiatives:

- Data exploration
- Data profiling and auditing
- Data cataloging

Data discovery is a diagnostic phase concerned with documenting the data in your organization and the characteristics of that data. Data discovery arms you with information about the accuracy, consistency, and reliability of your data. This information is essential in helping you determine what data is available in your organization and the validity and usability of that data to support the objectives of your organization.

Data discovery is based on the same principles that your doctor uses when you are sick. When he enters the room, he won't immediately say, "Well, we'd better give you an antibiotic." Instead, the doctor goes through a series of diagnostic tests and questions to determine the problem—checking your pulse, your blood pressure, and performing some blood work. After a thorough diagnostic review in which the doctor has eliminated irrelevant diagnoses and has pinpointed the problem, he is ready to move forward with the treatment.

> Data discovery has several components to it, and each prepares you for your data initiatives:
> 1. Data exploration
> 2. Data profiling and auditing
> 3. Data cataloging

Data exploration involves the finding and compiling of information from your IT infrastructure. This is essentially a compilation of metadata from various data sources into a single environment that provides a unified view of all available data. This can be done in a variety of ways—from documenting on a sheet of paper, to compiling information in a spreadsheet, to using a data exploration tool to capture and manipulate the metadata. No matter how you do it, just be sure you do it.

Data profiling and auditing takes you to the next level—actually looking at the data within the source systems and understanding the data elements and the anomalies. A thorough data profiling exercise will alert you to data that does not match the characteristics defined in the metadata compiled during data exploration. But, more important, data profiling can also tell you if the data meets your business needs (does it match the business rules that the business users define for the data?). In addition, with data profiling, you can determine the relationships across your data sources—where you have similar data, where data is in conflict, where data is duplicated, and where data may be dormant. Data profiling discovers the technical fit (does it match the documented structure of the data source?) and the business fit of the data (does it accommodate the needs of the business user?).

Some organizations have written their own tools to do data profiling, usually relying on very talented SQL (Structured Query Language) developers. These SQL programs are inflexible as they are developed to profile a very specific set of data. It is worth noting, however, that there are terrific data profiling technologies available today that can be deployed over your entire data inventory at a fraction of the cost and with better results than in-house development. One of the most important things you can do to ensure the long-term health of your data—and your organization—is to invest in data profiling technology.

Additionally, data discovery requires **data cataloging**. The goal of cataloging the data is to create a single source of information that has both **technical** and **business** information about data across your entire organization. You need a development environment where data sources can be combined and rationalized: a place where you can group data sources into projects to allow you to work across your data sources and develop a consistent environment for manipulating your data and executing your data-intensive applications. The data cataloging phase is also an opportunity to add metadata—especially business metadata—about your data sources. This allows you to answer some important questions:

- What does the data mean?
- How was the data collected?
- How has the data been transformed?

The answers to these questions will be essential in later phases of the life-cycle. The ultimate goal of data cataloging is to create a data dictionary, a comprehensive environment that documents:

- Data sources
- The technical characteristics of the data
- The relationships of data across the organization
- Who is responsible for the data (both the business stakeholder as well as the IT application that manages the data)
- The business definition of the data
- Any special information about how the data was derived or calculated

Cataloging the data and creating the data dictionary creates the one place that you can go to see all the data in your organization and its value to the organization. The data dictionary is a complete document for one of your most important corporate assets—your data.

Data discovery tasks are split between IT and the business—with the data stewards acting as the go-between to ensure that both IT and business are operating toward the same goal. IT is normally responsible for data exploration and for compiling an environment that provides access to data sources. However, the business analysts are the ones who understand the data, the meaning of the data, and whether the data is appropriate for the needs of the business. Data discovery is a joint activity and it is a great entry point for both business and IT to begin collaboration efforts.

DESIGN

After completing Step 1 of the data management lifecycle, you will be able to identify sources, understand the underlying formats and structures, and assess the relationships and uses of data across the organization. Now you face another challenge—taking all of these different structures and formats, data sources, and data feeds, and creating an environment that accommodates the needs of your business. This accommodation requires consolidation and coordination, all the while concentrating on three major areas:

1. Consistency of rules
2. Consistency of the data model that describes your organization
3. Consistency of business processes

One of the most important inventions of all time is the mechanical clock. Before the advent of the mechanical clock, there was no distinction between events and time. Time was measured by an event start and an event end. There was no co-ordination of activities, no real opportunity to plan beyond "when the sun comes up" or "when the sun sets." The mechanical clock allowed people to have a single frame of reference. Over time, clocks started to coordinate the activities of people around the world. Thanks to this invention, we now know

> Major areas of data design:
> 1. Consistency of rules
> 2. Consistency of the data model that describes your organization
> 3. Consistency of business processes

when to wake up, when to show up for work, and when to drop our children off at school. A clock gives us a single frame of reference allowing events to be coordinated with respect to time.

The design phase of the data management lifecycle methodology provides the same concept for organizations that the mechanical clock did for time—it provides a single frame of reference so that the entire organization can work from a coordinated view. As depicted in Figure 12.2, the goal of the design phase is to provide a single definition of data elements, a single set of business rules, and a single environment to manage and govern data.

During the design phase, organizations tend to make two major mistakes. The first mistake is that they try to accomplish too much all at once. Remember, data governance projects are based on improving a business initiative. The scope of the initial design should be just enough to satisfy the needs of that project. After a single phase is completed, the scope of the design is broadened to accommodate the needs of the next business

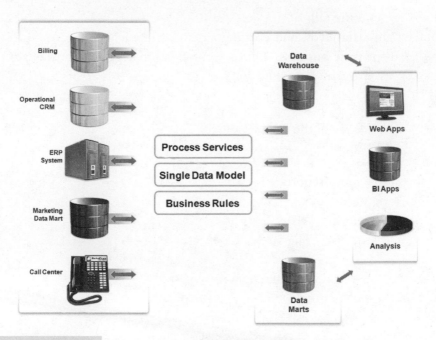

FIGURE 12.2   Blueprint of the design phase of the data
management lifecycle methodology

initiative. Keep in mind, you do not design in phases—you implement in phases. Think globally, act locally.

The second mistake organizations make is to leave the design phase up to the IT professionals. Just because a project is titled "data model consistency" or "business rule creation," this does not mean that IT makes all the decisions. In reality, IT becomes more involved in Step 3: Enablement. The goal of design is to have your rules and models map to the needs of your business. This is something only business users can successfully accomplish.

The design phase encompasses the establishment of a single frame of reference by providing a single data model, a single set of business rules, and a single set of business processes. Before starting the design phase, you should take care to limit your efforts to a single business initiative and complete the data discovery phase to better understand the landscape. Now, you are ready to design a data model that reflects the needs of the organization. This can be challenging—again, not from a *technology* perspective, but from a *people* perspective. The data model is the single, definitive source for how your data maps to your business. Because of this relationship, there must be agreement on the most basic issues. Take a customer definition, for example:

- How do you determine customers? Who is a customer? Existing customers only? Past customers? Prospects? Marketing contacts?

- Looking at the various customer systems (CRM, ERP, sales force automation [SFA], finance, and so on), where are the best attributes? Where is the best source of phone number, address, and historical purchases? What attributes are needed to properly define the customer?

- Is every contact at a company a customer? Or is the customer actually the entire company with various contacts scattered across several departments? How do you manage corporate hierarchies where one company owns another company? Do you care?

This is only the beginning of the type of questions you need to consider, and these are not easy questions to answer. They are not the kind of questions IT can answer. The data steering committee proposes the model definition, and then the data stewards check the validity with respect to their areas of responsibility. Ultimately, a model that should accommodate the needs of everyone will be achieved.

The process of establishing business rules is much like the process for establishing the data model. Business rules are ultimately determined by business users through a process of defining and then validating across the lines of business. Ultimately, an organization needs one set of business rules that can be stored centrally but deployed across all data sources, applications and lines of business. We will look at this more in Step 3: Enablement. Trying to reach agreement on business rules can be as tough as trying to reach a consensus on what the data model should look like. For customer business rules, for example, hard decisions have to be made:

- What is the discounting policy for customers?
- Who owns the customer account (that is, how are sales territories defined)?
- How are our customers and prospects segmented?

Organizations can have thousands of business rules. Many of those are not documented and most are not automated. The design phase provides a consistent method of defining and documenting these business rules.

Finally, we should look at the consistency of business processes. As you attempt to improve a business initiative, you will find processes that will be affected by the changes you are making. During the business plan and discovery phase, you will identify processes that are potentially impacted. Now, the task is to provide consistency across these processes. I know it seems odd, but the goal of improved data management is not to have better data—it is to provide better execution of business processes through optimization and automation. Think of an organization with hundreds or thousands of business processes that are executed every day. Only 5 to 15 percent of those processes are automated. The rest require intervention or human action. This results in inconsistencies and nonoptimal execution. However, the answers to these inconsistencies lie in the data—accurate and

> The goal of improved data management is not to have better data—it is to provide better execution of business processes.

trusted data. It ensures consistent and optimal execution. Data services will answer questions across the application, such as:

- Is this a new customer or an existing customer?
- Is this customer in good standing (have they paid their bills?)?
- When was the last time we contacted this customer?

To maximize efficiency, you should have one process that answers these types of questions regardless of whether the question is being asked by applications designed for finance, sales, marketing, or any other business unit. The design phase ensures consistency across your organization.

ENABLE

As you move from the discovery/design phases to the enablement phase, the primary responsibility shifts from the business users to the IT staff. Now that the business users have established how the data and rules should be defined, it is up to the IT staff to ensure that databases and applications adhere to the definitions.

There are many enablement architectures: enabling ERP and CRM applications via proprietary interfaces; enabling data marts and data warehouses via extraction, transformation, and loading (ETL) flows; enabling master data management (MDM) systems via service-oriented architecture (SOA)/ETL or other technologies. The method and management of enabling the data in any of these environments is a decision that IT has to make in order to ensure the integrity and integration into the various systems.

One of the biggest mistakes companies make in the enablement phase is to duplicate the rules and standards that came out of Step 2 for each application or data source. This would be analogous to having the telephone but not having the phone network. Although the telephone is a great invention, it is actually the telephone network that makes it practical. Without the network, each telephone would have to be connected directly to another telephone—ultimately making the telephone a cumbersome and impractical device. But the telephone network—initially made up of copper wires connected to other copper wires, and more recently, cell towers connected to other cell towers connected to satellites—has made the telephone ubiquitous. In IT deployments, though, we tend to operate more like the telephone without the network. We implement a unique interface to various systems, duplicating the rules and definitions for each system we interface. Ultimately, we end up with many point-to-point interfaces that must be maintained and modified each time a rule or business initiative changes. This approach is highly impractical. A better solution is to build the definitions once and ensure that you have the ability to deploy those definitions across your organization. A phrase that I have heard many organizations use over the past decade is "We want to build our standards and rules once and then have the ability to use them repeatedly and propagate to the entire organization seamlessly."

Regardless of the technology being used to enable the data environment, you must approach the project in a methodical fashion. In Part Four, I will talk more about technology options and issues. For now, we will concentrate on the process. For each data source, each business process and each application that is modified to the new data definitions, you will need to:

- Understand the requirements.
- Validate that the new integration meets the requirements.
- Deploy the interface into production.

Applications and systems have been built over the years to meet the requirements of users. When we move to modify the landscape to provide consistent data across our organizations, we can jeopardize these requirements. Before you begin any integration project, know the requirements, such as the service-level requirements imposed by both IT and the business user community. Any modifications to the systems must be done without a negative impact on the service level.

There are two types of validation that must be done before deploying. First, you must ensure that all service-level requirements are met. Second, you must validate that the new rules and definitions you designed in Step 2 are being accurately reflected. One important aspect of this is to devote adequate time to testing. It is not glamorous, nor flashy, but it can be the difference between success and failure. The National Institute of Standards and Technology estimates that 80 percent of the development time will be on finding and fixing errors.[2] Do not underestimate this testing step.

After completing these tasks, you will be ready to deploy into the new environment, knowing that one more part of your organization is now operating with consistent, accurate and reliable data and processes.

MAINTAIN

Your data systems are like anything else that you want to continue to run effectively. You must constantly monitor the environment, checking and validating that things are working correctly. When I take my car into the shop for the standard service, there are more than 50 checks performed. *Each time*. But the checking does not stop there. There are also computers throughout the car that are constantly monitoring and recording activity. This data is then fed to a central collection computer. If something is not right with my car, the repair shop can remotely access this data source and diagnose any systems that are not running normally. This same rigor needs to be applied to your data environment.

All too often, organizations take the attitude that all the work for a system or application is in the initial development. This attitude of "do it once and you're done" is one of the major obstacles to an efficiently running data management environment. A successful data management lifecycle requires constant vigilance and continuous care.

A healthy data lifecycle requires a robust monitoring and reporting system. The data needs to be consistently monitored to ensure it remains fit-for-purpose for your organization. You may be asking yourself why this is so critically important. After all, you just spent lots of time, energy, and resources to get your systems to a point where the business users have a consistent and validated view of your organization. Isn't it time to just enjoy the success of all this effort? Quite the opposite. Very few organizations are static—they are forever growing and evolving. For example, you sign on new partners that bring new data to the table. You hire new employees that are not indoctrinated into the quality culture, and they make mistakes. Your business changes, sales regions are created or modified, you take on new initiatives, or you develop new products. All of these have to be reflected in your data.

> A successful data management lifecycle requires constant vigilance and continuous care.

It is remarkable how quickly things change. In fact, at the very moment you deploy your coordinated and consistent data across your organization, things will be changing. Your mantra for success at this point needs to be (1) Monitor, (2) Report, and (3) Optimize. And, like everything else I have discussed, this needs to be as automated as possible. Data should be monitored and validated as it enters your organization to ensure that it is meeting your rules. And those rules need to be constantly monitored to ensure they are still meeting the needs of your business. Sounds like a lot of work. Luckily, by adopting a methodical approach to data management, you are in the best possible position to meet the needs of change. Efforts in discovery, design, and enablement allow you to consolidate the rules and requirements into a single environment. With only one place to go to make any changes to the data rules, the change can be immediately propagated across the organization. This is extremely important. Consider something as basic as a sales territory change. Unless you can coordinate the change across sales, marketing, and finance, you could run into many problems. For example, who is supposed to answer a customer's problem? How do you ascertain commissions and bonuses? Bad coordination can even impact the delivery of product to your customer ("No, that was your job" or "Nope. That's your territory."). Unless the change can be coordinated, it is not clear who has the responsibility to perform certain tasks.

The best way to ensure continuous return on your data management investments is to constantly monitor and optimize the systems to ensure that the data continues to reflect your business needs. Monitoring is a joint activity between IT and business users. IT sets up the monitors and validates that systems are running within their required service-level needs. Business users, though, benefit mostly from the monitoring reports—constantly reviewing the reports and validating that the data continues to reflect the needs of the organization.

ARCHIVE

One thing is certain in today's information age: Data will continue to pour into your organization. It is easy to see why it is important to be able to recognize when data is valuable to your organization. However, it is also important to recognize when data is no longer of interest to your organization. It is just as important to methodically retire that data when appropriate.

Archiving may be a bit of a misnomer for the final step in the data management lifecycle methodology. In reality, the process is closer to *reassessing* data. You may recognize that the requirements on your data have changed but the data is still useful. These observations will come directly from the monitoring activities in Step 4. In the event the data is still useful, but no longer meets your immediate needs—you need to go back to Step 1 and start the process over again. In the event that data is no longer useful to your organization, you must be able to retire the data appropriately. This allows you to free up resources—people and technology—that are being expended on maintaining the data environment. Let's look at what has happened in the financial services market sector. Financial institutions have folded or been sold in pretty large numbers. If you have data on a company that has gone out of business, or become part of another entity, you need to make decisions on eliminating or recategorizing that data. You do not want to spend resources managing the data of a company that no longer exists.

The data management lifecycle becomes more valuable the more widespread it is practiced. It is not until every data initiative consistently follows the lifecycle and manages data consistently that you will reap the full benefits of your data. Of course, the best way to get adoption and acceptance of the lifecycle is to publicize your successes—advertise the benefits to your organization. When you began your lifecycle, you were solving a business problem. By the time you have reached this phase in the lifecycle, you should have improved your business. Communicate and evangelize this! Let it be known that the efforts were successful and the business is improved. This is the way to ensure funding for the next iteration—solving the next business problem.

Adherence to the quality culture is an ongoing activity that requires the continuous diligence of people across your organization. The quality culture needs to be embraced, and adherence needs to be enforced. I have worked with a number of companies as they have developed their quality culture. There are two in particular that have embraced the concept of gaining and maintaining participation. The two companies had very different ways of doing this. The first company is a high tech company that embarked on the quality culture path because inconsistent reports hampered solid decision making and executives were frustrated that they could not trust the reports presented to them. The inconsistencies were pervasive—preventing the organization from answering the most basic questions, like "How many customers do we have?" and "What were our sales figures last quarter?" You would think these would be easy questions to answer, but you'd be surprised how few companies can answer questions like this correctly and with confidence. In this particular company, they developed a quality culture that has been adopted by most of the organization. They followed the data governance principles I have outlined in this chapter. It was not an overnight success, but they started down the path and saw their processes improve over time. Now, the effort has been so successful that all reports and data files must be validated against the policies of the quality culture. In fact, they have adopted an actual seal—a physical stamp—that goes on reports that have been generated from the data managed by the policies of the quality culture. Management will not even consider a report that does not bear this seal. All reports and data files used for everything from financial systems to decision support are based only on approved and trusted data.

The second organization took a very different approach. It was a more punitive approach, but just as effective. This organization has what it calls the Quality Wall of Shame. Every week, the Wall of Shame contains the names of the individuals or departments that have violated the quality culture. Every Monday morning when people arrive at work, they immediately check the Wall of Shame, hoping their names and departments do not appear on it. It is one more method used to assure a constant focus on quality. However, the method involves more than just having pride that your name is not on the wall. Employee compensation is actually based on ability to work within the quality culture and to stay off the Wall of Shame.

I hope that you have seen why a methodical, step-by-step approach to managing your data is the best approach. As your business needs dictate, systems must be incorporated into the quality culture. Any new data, system, or application must adhere to this data management lifecycle methodology. Only then will your data truly become a corporate asset.

The quality culture part began with some wisdom from Aristotle, "Quality is not an act, it is a habit." Good habits are best learned by repetitive execution. Your data lifecycle process may be a bit different from the one I have outlined—it may have fewer steps, or it may have more. The important thing, though, is that you have a data management lifecycle process in place and that your organization execute according to that process. Only through repetition of the lifecycle will you gain full control over your data. And with that control, you will be able to use your data to better your organization.

WHAT'S NEXT?

In this part, I discussed the people and processes that help organizations implement the lifecycle of data. A lifecycle is the same regardless of the systems and applications that use the data; but the sophistication of the lifecycle process increases as a company climbs the Data Governance Maturity Model (described in Part Two). Hopefully this part helped you get an understanding for the quality culture, how it needs to be implemented, and how to take a methodical approach toward achieving a quality culture in your organization.

As we discussed, people and processes make the quality culture possible. Having the right people in the right roles with a single goal is the essential first step. Defining these positions and responsibilities will get things started. Altering your processes for robust, repeatable results is also critical, and adherence to these processes will ensure the viability of your data. When the people and processes are in place, you are ready for the third critical aspect of the quality culture—technology.

In Part Four, I look at the technology that will be required for successful data governance and data management. Implementing a quality culture requires the successful synthesis of people, process, and technology. The proper use of technology is essential for you to effectively manage the ever-increasing amount of data required in today's information age. How, and when, you apply technology will depend on the capacity of your organization to understand and implement the right technology in the right place at the right time.

I have a friend who is multitalented when it comes to carpentry, home improvement projects, and electronics. He builds his own cabinets, tiles his kitchen and bathroom (he even tiled the floor of his garage), fixes his cars, and does all of his home repairs. He has every tool and gadget that any repairman might need. His storage shed is overflowing with table saws and miter saws, hand tools and power tools, electric tools and pneumatic tools. He uses them all and uses them well. I am not so much of a handyman. I can do some basic repairs, so I only need the tools that are required for basic repairs. For example, I do not have a table saw or any pneumatic tools. I do not need them because I do not have the skills to use them. Until I have acquired those skills, purchasing a table saw would be a waste of time and money—and dangerous.

Whenever a home-building project goes awry, I tend to blame the tools. I think, *If I only had the same tools as my friend, I would be much more successful.* Of course, I know that's not really the case. I just do not have the skills and knowledge to accomplish everything I would like to do. When a solution does not work, the first impulse is to blame the technology. While there are certainly technologies that do not work, failures normally result from organizations not matching their technology purchases to their stage of data maturity.

The same dynamic exists when it comes to the principles for managing your data. Sophisticated solutions to improve data quality are useless if a company does not have the people and processes in place to consistently run data through the data management lifecycle methodology. A data quality or data integration technology is merely a reflection of the quality culture (or lack thereof) within the organization. The maturity model, then, helps you understand both the business applications that can benefit them and which associated technologies are useful to guide the collection and management of data. Part Four will help you understand how to best map technology to the needs and maturity of your organization.

■ **NOTES**

1. National Environmental Health Association, "Position Regarding Sale or Distribution of Raw Milk," January 28, 2008.
2. NIST (National Institute of Standards and Technology) Publication #2002-10, June 2002.

Closing the Loop: Selecting the Right Technology for Your Organization

CHAPTER 13

Undisciplined Organizations: Discovering the Value of Data Quality Tools

Bad habits are like a comfortable bed—easy to get into and hard to get out of.

—PROVERB

EXECUTIVE OVERVIEW

Undisciplined companies need to view technology as a tool. As much as business improvement guides focus on integrating data between business units and breaking down barriers, undisciplined organizations need to take baby steps, focusing instead on allowing individuals within different departments the opportunity to test data management technologies that address their specific needs. These organizations are not ready to find success with business applications like customer relationship management (CRM), enterprise resource planning (ERP), or master data management (MDM). Instead, the undisciplined organization should focus on applications that can benefit the most from more department-driven, function-specific technology implementations such as:

(continued)

(Continued)

- Database marketing
- Sales force automation (SFA)
- Spend management

In this chapter, organizations will learn about data profiling, data quality, and identity resolution—the three data management technologies that will help undisciplined companies succeed at these department-driven efforts.

Remember

1. Data quality and data governance should *never* be considered a one-time project. A quality culture must be established as an ongoing, continuous process.

2. No organization can tackle enterprise-wide data quality and data governance all at once. To be successful, your journey must be evolutionary. Start small and take achievable steps that can be measured along the way.

As described in Part Two, undisciplined companies are like firefighters trying to contain a brush fire—scrambling from one hot zone to the next. There is no time to look at the big picture, even if the executives had the time and inclination to do so. Data has been mismanaged for years, and it often takes a cataclysmic event—like the fire at the plumbing company discussed in the first chapter—to get executives to pay attention.

The Rapid Pace of Technology

Technology is changing fast to better support the rapid change of business. It is imperative for us, regardless of our level of corporate maturity, to select the technologies that are right for us. As we look back over time, we have seen an evolution of technology. In the last decade alone, we have seen evolution from proprietary mainframe applications to data warehouses for cross-functional consolidation to distributed computing to packaged ERP and CRM systems to help organizations benefit from the experience of others to master data management and business process automation technologies for more consistent business execution.

Of course, the list goes on and on. The hope is that the application of technology will help all of us improve our business—our ability to generate revenue, control costs, and mitigate risks.

Even today, we see the introduction of new technologies available to us occurring at a dizzying pace. The advent of the service-oriented architecture has been expanded beyond the internal infrastructure of an organization to the broader infrastructure of the internet. This has created a cottage industry that will grow into a formidable computing environment—cloud computing. Cloud computing will revolutionize how and where you manage your applications. But, like ERP, CRM, data warehousing, or master data management, cloud computing is just another technology evolution that help us more cheaply and efficiently run our businesses.

Different technologies may or may not be right for you. It is important for you to understand how technology can be adopted by your organization and what advantage technologies can bring to your organization. Remember, though, that all of these different technologies have one thing in common: your data. Whether a proprietary system, an on-premise ERP system, a cloud-based CRM system, or data warehouse, it is your data that will make these applications useful to your business and it is the data that will make these environments work well together.

COPING AND THRIVING AS AN UNDISCIPLINED ORGANIZATION

Even with executive understanding, undisciplined organizations struggle to find success with business applications like CRM or ERP. Unfortunately, many undisciplined companies have tried and failed to do just that. Undisciplined companies often view an IT application as a panacea, a shortcut to more simplified, unified view of the enterprise. Yet, the failures keep mounting. Technology alone cannot solve business problems. Technology, together with the required changes in process and behavior, moves organizations to more effective use of their data, which in turn drives their organizations forward.

Undisciplined companies normally operate as a number of discrete and nonintegrated departments and lines of business. While this is not ideal, it is fact. It also has advantages because there are business and IT experts that have very strong skill sets, albeit ones that are limited in scope. The undisciplined organization needs to take advantage of these skills and allow these lines of business to make positive strides to address their specific needs. This serves two purposes:

1. The company can yield some immediate results from quality data, even in isolated pockets.

2. The initial technology program will help deliver the first of many data management strategies that can ultimately lead to a more comprehensive data governance effort.

In order for undisciplined organizations to improve, they need to be aware of what it will take to move along the maturity model. This is done by identifying the right business issues at the functional level. At the same time, they must implement the data management foundation that will help the organization as a whole. Typically, undisciplined organizations will implement applications that benefit primarily a single department or functional area. For example, common applications for an undisciplined organization include:

- Database marketing
- Sales force automation
- Spend management

Each of these efforts typically impact only one or two departments. Database marketing and sales force automation will be utilized by marketing and sales, while spend management is the domain of procurement and operations. A data management program, initially with data quality technology to provide some support for improving the data within these applications, is appropriate for these companies.

Until the mid-1990s, almost all companies were in this category, and there are still many organizations or parts of organizations that are still working with outdated tools and processes. My local cable company provides a variety of services: Internet services, high-definition TV, digital recording, and digital phone. And I contract them for most of these services. Yet you would not believe how often I get flyers from them asking me to sign up for services that I already have. Companies spend millions of dollars to print and mail those catalogs and flyers. We will usually get multiple versions of the flyers—one to me and one to my wife—an over-sight caused by multiple versions of the household in their database marketing application. This is a simple case of sales and marketing operating as discrete silos and the lack of attention to the quality of the data in these silos. However, as progress is made in eliminating this business improving practices, the benefits—even to undisciplined organizations—of applications of data quality and data management technology are evident.

The problems with undisciplined organizations will continue if they fail to develop a good understanding of their current situation—and the best way out of it. Marketing departments in undisciplined organizations often outsource their reduplication efforts. By doing this, they are missing an opportunity to get a better understanding of their data. If the outsourcing is done frequently it may make financial sense to bring the process in-house. If it is done infrequently, thousands of dollars are wasted between the cleanings, because each month two percent of data becomes out of date because of death, divorce, marriage, and or moves.[1] And not all consumer organizations have focused on organizing and cleaning data by household—something critical to eliminating duplicates caused by multiple people in the same household who all have a relationship with the organization.

Similarly, sales force automation technology is designed to help organizations understand the relationship they have with their customers and prospects. If the data is not well managed, customers will get multiple sales pitches from different people within the same organization. The organization will not understand the full relationship they have with their customers. SFA applications can also increase productivity among sales people, track sales leads, and create sales forecasts. None of the promises are viable, however, if the data is skewed. For instance, if a company's products do not have standard names (one salesperson enters a sale under one name and another calls it something different), the company does not really know who is selling what to whom. There must also be a way to coherently reorganize data when sales territories are rearranged. All of these require attention to the quality of the data.

Spend management is another area where undisciplined organizations benefit from data management technologies and begin to learn how to use data to improve their organizations. Spend management is the process of understanding what you buy, from whom you buy, and how to save money by buying products at the right time from the right supplier. Most organizations do not have a good understanding of what they buy. They buy the same products from various suppliers, they buy incompatible products, and they buy products when they do not need those products. All of these issues can be traced back to poor data management of purchase patterns and suppliers. Most undisciplined organizations buy products as they need them from whatever supplier seems most convenient. By completely understanding what the entire organization is purchasing, the organization can consolidate purchases, better manage the delivery of purchases, and demand discounts by buying all similar products from a single supplier.

Certainly, undisciplined organizations are also just starting on their journey to make their data a corporate asset, even if they can only do it one department or function at a time. The key to doing this is to understand the data in their environments. Only by understanding the data assets can the undisciplined organization begin to make progress on the necessary data initiatives to improve their business. Technologies to discover, assess, and improve their data are key initiatives. As they begin to make their data work for them, there are several technologies they need to utilize:

Three of the most important data management technologies that undisciplined companies need to adopt are:

1. Data profiling.
2. Data quality.
3. Identity resolution.

> Three of the most important data management technologies that undisciplined companies need to adopt are:
> 1. Data profiling
> 2. Data quality
> 3. Identity resolution

DATA PROFILING

Data profiling is a fundamental step that should begin every data-driven initiative, yet it is often not done, or companies assume that profiling has been done already. Engaging in any data management initiative without a clear understanding of these issues will lead to large development and cost overruns or potential project failures. The effect can be incredibly costly. For example, one company I worked with spent more than $100,000 in labor costs identifying and correcting 111 different spellings of the company AT&T. Data problems within your organization can lead to substandard customer relations, wasted expenses, poor decisions, lost sales, and, ultimately, failed businesses.

Remember, profiling your data is based on the same principle that your mechanic uses when you take your car to the shop. If you tell the mechanic that the car has trouble starting, the mechanic first goes through a series of diagnostic steps to determine the problem. After a thorough diagnostic review, the mechanic validates the reliability of each relevant part and is ready to make the needed changes. With data profiling, you can also look under the hood to gain valuable insight into your business processes, refine these procedures over time, and recommend new ways to refine and enhance the data entry and data collection processes.

Although excellent technology tools and methodologies exist today, many organizations continue to conduct data profiling tasks manually— or they ignore profiling altogether. Manual profiling may be practical when there are very few columns and minimal rows to profile. But organizations today have thousands of columns and millions (or billions) of records. Profiling this data manually would require an inordinate amount of human intervention that would still be error-prone and subjective.

In practice, your organization needs a data profiling tool that can automatically process data from any data source and process hundreds or thousands of columns across many data sources. Data profiling and data discovery are the two most important phases of data discovery for the undisciplined organization.

The first part of this process is to identify data that is similar or related in nature. Using data discovery tools on your applications will help you understand where you keep data about customers or products or employees. This information can be used to help you map relationships between different data sources. Knowing the landscape of your data is crucial to the analysis, quality, and identity resolution steps that follow. Data discovery can be done by hand for initiatives that are very limited in scope. More practically, though, a data discovery tool should be used to pull information from the various applications and allow you to manage and work with those applications in a cohesive fashion.

Data profiling (or data analysis) is another key part of the profiling process. In order to achieve a high degree of quality control, routine audits of your data are essential. A sample list of these audits follows, along with an example of each.

Type of Audit	Example
Domain checking	In a gender field, the value should be M or F.
Range checking	For age, the value should be less than 125 and greater than 0.
Cross-field verification	If a customer orders an upgrade, make sure that customer already owns the product to be upgraded.
Address format verification	If "Street" is the designation for street, then make sure no other designations are used.
Name standardization	If "Robert" is the standard name for Robert, then make sure Bob, Robt. and Rob are not used.
Basic statistics, frequencies, ranges, and outliers	If a company has products that cost between $1,000 and $10,000, you can run a report for product prices that occur outside of this range. You can also view product information, such as SKU codes, to see if the SKU groupings are correct and in line with expected frequencies.
Duplicate identification	If an inactive flag is used to identify customers that are no longer covered by health benefits, make sure duplicate customer records are marked inactive.
Data rule compliance	If closed credit accounts must have a balance of zero, make sure there are no records where the closed account flag is true and the account balance total is greater than zero.

Another concept to keep in mind when practicing these data discovery and profiling techniques is to adhere to the methodology. Data profiling is the first step in the data quality integration process that helps you diagnose your enterprise problems. But it is not a one-and-done project, something that you can apply once and be done with it. Proper data profiling must be part of a larger data quality methodology that ties these processes together in a cohesive fashion through an integrated and phased approach. These phases, or building blocks of data quality, begin with data profiling and continue with data quality (standardizing, validating, and verifying your data), data integration (accessing, linking, and connecting data from multiple sources), data enrichment (augmenting and enhancing your data), and data monitoring (continually examining and auditing your data based on prebuilt business rules). But before you can begin the improvement phases, you have to know the quality of your existing data. For example, for a "State" field, you may think that a "State" field is always represented as a two character abbreviation. You may also think that "State" is fairly evenly distributed. A quick profile report (see Figure 13.1) can help you make quick observations, some of which may surprise you.

With data profiling technology, you can quickly determine the characteristics of your data, and then continue with the data quality and data improvement.

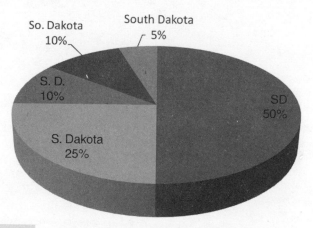

FIGURE 13.1   **State Frequency Distribution**

DATA QUALITY

Data quality is about cleansing your data of faulty, misleading elements that cost your company money and customers and can ultimately be embarrassing for your organization. For example, a data quality tool can help you quickly cleanse an address list of prospective customers, weeding out dead addresses or addresses of existing customers. Data quality uses a combination of data standardization, data rationalization, and data transformations to ensure that the data in and across databases and applications is consistent.

Data problems abound in most organizations. Some of the more common problems today include outdated, inconsistent, missing, orphaned (data that becomes separated from the other relevant data supporting it), or duplicated data; data anomalies or outliers (data that is statistically distant from the rest of the data); and data that does not meet specified business rules. Before you begin any data quality improvement initiative, you should ask and address some key questions:

- Do you trust the quality of the data you are using in this initiative?
- Does the data for this initiative conform to the business rules monitoring process you expect to set up later?
- Will the existing data support the needed functionality?
- Is the data you are using complete enough to execute your data initiative?

Engaging in any data initiative without a clear understanding of these issues will lead to large development and cost overruns or potential project failures.

Data quality technology typically follows the blueprint provided by a data profiling tool. Profiling finds the problem, and data quality technology allows you to create rules to fix this data. Data quality technology can help you:

- Plan and prioritize data correction initiatives to begin to build more consistent, accurate, and reliable data.
- Parse data into separate components to help identify and resolve problematic data.

- Standardize, correct, and normalize data to create a more unified view of corporate information.

- Verify and validate data accuracy to improve the overall accuracy of customer records, product data, and other information.

- Apply business rules across the enterprise to ensure all corporate data reflects business needs.

There are a number of different tactics employed during this phase. Some of the most commonly employed measures include:

- **Data standardization to correct multiple permutations of data.** For example, ACME Manufacturing Corporation may be represented in the same data source as Acme Mfg. Corp, ACME, and ACME Manufacturing.

- **Pattern standardization to create valid patterns of data across tables and columns.** Some pieces of data, such as phone numbers or tax ID numbers, are found in easily recognized variant patterns. Others, such as product or item data, may have different standards across industries or companies. Pattern standardization can take information in nonstandard formats and transform it into an accepted standard format.

- **Address verification to confirm that addresses are valid and actionable.** One common issue in databases is incorrect city, state, and postal code combinations. A software solution that can determine if the city and state match the entered postal code is critical for accurate address information. By searching postal data, your software solution should be able to locate the proper postal code and change the record to create an accurate address.

- **Adherence to business rules.** Data is used across your organization to ensure that the data meets the needs of the business. Often, though, different parts of the organization use different metrics, calculations, and rules for the same business entity. Data quality technology will help ensure consistency across the organization.

In the following example, the inventory level for a lawn mower with a product name of "KS63C" appears to be 19 units. A user reviewing the

Product	Inventory Amount
KS63C WB Mower	100
KS63C	19
Walk-Behind Mower - KS63C	30

KS63C WB Mower	KS63C Walk-Behind Mower
KS63C	KS63C Walk-Behind Mower
Walk-Behind Mower - KS63C	KS63C Walk-Behind Mower

KS63C Walk-Behind Mower	149

FIGURE 13.2   Data quality technology provides a better understanding of product inventory

raw data could identify that the inventory levels for this product is in reality 149 units by including other data points that have similar codes. Without a data quality solution, however, any computer-generated report that asks for products with the code "KS63C" might yield only 19 results. (See Figure 13.2.)

Data quality technology helps you transform inconsistent data into one common product representation. In this example, product data is standardized by converting each instance of similar data into a consistent naming pattern: "KS36C Walk-Behind Mower." This allows your reporting and application software to show the true picture—and will generate a result. in the appropriate inventory levels of 149 units.

The specific approach taken may differ for each data element, and the decision on the approach falls to the business area responsible for the data. It is also important to note that the data quality activity improves the existing data but does not address the root cause of the data problems. If the enterprise is truly interested in improving data quality, it must also investigate the reasons that the data contained errors and then initiate appropriate actions, including incentives and changes to business procedures to improve future data.

With data quality, organizations have enacted the measures to bring the completeness and accuracy of the data in each source to acceptable levels.

IDENTITY RESOLUTION

Identity resolution is the lynchpin for everything from knowing your customer, to data consolidations, to regulatory compliance. Headlines during the 2008 U.S. elections about problems matching new voter registrations to databases like those maintained by the U.S. Social Security Administration and by state motor vehicle registries point to the critical need for identity resolution technology. In one U.S. state, one-third of about 600,000 new voter registrations were flagged as potential mismatches. In questioning whether each discrepancy needed to be investigated prior to the election, that state's top election official election officials claimed typographical errors were the problem. The state did not have the technology tools to quickly conclude that a John K. Smith at 100 Ohio Street was the same as John Smith at 100 East Ohio Street in the database. This made it difficult to determine if there were valid new voters or if something akin to fraud was occurring.

For any type of data, different data elements about the same item will often exist in multiple databases across applications or within the same database or application. Identity management is useful when organizations attempt to rationalize data across different sources. Identity management provides the ability to take these divergent pieces of information and unify them within a single master record.

Take the example of the company that had two product files: a master product file extracted from its U.S.-based subsidiary and another from the product database in Europe. The company sold the same products in both areas, but the products were listed in each database by different names. Product identification numbers were different in Europe from those in the United States, even though the products were identical. The result was that the company had no real idea about their total inventory of finished products.

The first challenge in data integration is to recognize that the same products exist in each of the two sources—the process of linking. The second challenge is to combine the data into a single view of the product—the process of consolidation.

Identity management recognized a product description that was common to both files. The U.S. file contained the description, brand name, and a product identifier all in one field and in various patterns. The European file contained European product descriptions, also with varied patterns and abbreviations. The product descriptions, patterns, and abbreviations were inconsistent across the databases. To uncover the connection, data identity resolution technology was used to:

- Parse the description from both databases into product-specific attributes and into a brand name.
- Reconcile the differences in brand names.
- Reconcile the differences in product attributes (short forms, abbreviations, and so on).
- Standardize the brand names and attributes.
- Merge databases by matching standardized names and attributes.
- Display reports of matching products.

After data integration, the company was able to leverage a comprehensive view of all the data known about its products. The same principles and techniques may be applied to any type of data to create integrated master records. While it is easy to visualize the way this exercise could be done by a human, identity resolution technology allows for the matching to be done in an automated fashion by using techniques similar to human thought processes.

Identity resolution goes beyond cleansing databases of obvious duplications. With this technology, companies can determine less obvious duplications and synchronize individual records. For any organization with regulatory burdens, identity resolution is a must. For example, almost every country maintains a list of designated individuals (terrorists, money launderers, drug traffickers) with which companies cannot do business. Matching your customers to the government watch lists is not a straightforward exercise. Most individuals on these lists are doing everything they can to ensure they are not identified. Identity resolution technology will look beyond the obvious matches and look for nonobvious relationships.

Identity resolution can also help organizations solve business problems, such as keeping a sales automation force solution up to date. Identity management solutions determine if customers listed in different sources are, in fact, the same customer—and intelligently integrates customer information from multiple applications and databases. With identity management, companies can flag potential matches within the IT infrastructure and isolate the best data from the various sources.

The next step is to take this identity management approach and apply it in real time to transactional data. After the initial data quality efforts, companies have consistent and accurate data within their customer databases. This process has developed a type of business logic at the data level for standardizing and matching information across business sources. Organizations can apply those same rules to new transactions—and uncover any that fail to meet compliance guidelines.

When your organization has addressed data profiling, data quality, and identity resolution within isolated applications like database marketing and SFA, you will have the understanding it takes to bring in more sophisticated business applications.

With undisciplined organizations, the key to maturing is to implement technologies that help you better understand your data. This is a foundation for improving specific functional areas, and is especially imperative as undisciplined organizations begin to mature.

■ NOTE

1. "Data Quality and the Bottom Line: Achieving Business Success through a Commitment to High Quality Data," The Data Warehousing Institute, Report Series 2002.

CHAPTER 14

Reactive Organizations: Choose the Technology That Gets the Most from Your Applications

Life is like a piano . . . what you get out of it depends on how you play it.

—Tom Lehrer

Executive Overview

Reactive organizations build on the data quality tools and processes in place to successfully use data warehouses, enterprise resource planning (ERP), and customer relationship management (CRM) solutions. Reactive companies need data quality, profiling, and identify resolution tools. But now they also need:

- **Metadata exploration** to analyze the "data about the data" to answer those questions before bringing bad, unreliable, or ill-suited data into a new system.

- **Business rules monitoring** (also known as data validation) to answer the question: Are the data quality initiatives focused on the intent of the data? Just as ERP or CRM is the first move toward centralized business processes, business rules monitoring is the first step towards a codified data governance program.

(continued)

(Continued)

- **Data reconciliation** efforts to reconcile and resolve duplicate records across sources, preferably in near–real time. Data reconciliation often includes data quality, metadata tools, and other technologies.

REMEMBER

1. Data quality and data governance should *never* be considered a one-time project. A quality culture must be established as an ongoing, continuous process.

2. No organization can tackle enterprise-wide data quality and data governance all at once. To be successful, your journey must be evolutionary. Start small and take achievable steps that can be measured along the way.

A reactive organization understands that data problems have implications across the organization, especially if the organization has been attempting to integrate data across departmental and divisional lines. The typical reactive organization is trying hard to gather data in a more cross-functional way. For instance, if the data in the sales force automation system is analyzed against finance data, it helps if both entities agree on how to label a customer. Will XYZ Corp.'s international division be counted separately, or should it be grouped together with the parent company? This seems like a minor point, but how can finance rely on sales projections if sales counts the company separately and finance considers it one entity?

Most reactive companies are looking at implementing—or have already implemented—CRM and ERP applications. These systems are meant to optimize and consolidate business processes, and they are implemented with the idea of integrating functional areas of the business by defining processes. Data is a secondary consideration for most ERP and CRM implementations. These solutions have a history of problems that can be traced in many instances to poor-quality data. Organizations in the reactive stage need the following technologies to get their investments in CRM, ERP, and data warehouses working:

- **Data quality, profiling, and identity resolution technologies.** These concepts are critical to maturing of undisciplined organizations (Chapter 6) and they are equally critical to the success of reactive organizations. These technologies provide added value to the reactive organizations, especially when the technologies are in place *before* a data warehouse, ERP, or CRM project is undertaken. If an organization is not sure how these technologies work, it should try them on a discrete application like database marketing or sales force automation.

- **Metadata exploration.** A critical component of any data consolidation effort is delving into the data you have on hand, knowing where it is, how it relates to other data in your organization, and what it means from a business perspective. Metadata exploration looks at the data about the data to answer those questions before you bring bad, unreliable, or ill-suited data into a new system. For instance, one application might capture only a customer's name, address, and phone number without a direct extension. Another captures that information, plus e-mail address, a direct extension phone number, and the person's title. This information can lead to understanding complex data sources, which makes any data consolidation effort much easier to accomplish.

- **Business rules monitoring (also known as data validation).** This is designed to answer one seemingly simple, but often vexing, question: Will my data meet my business requirements now and in the future?

- **Data reconciliation.** A sophisticated effort to reconcile and resolve duplicate records across sources is critical. Data reconciliation often includes data quality, metadata tools, and other technologies, while adding more data access and data loading capabilities.

Since the goal of the reactive organization is to consolidate and streamline business processes, these organizations need to merge existing systems. Independent sales force automation and marketing database systems may be merged into a single CRM system. Independent financial systems and distribution systems may be merged into a single ERP. This streamlining of systems, applications, and processes can make an organization more efficient if the data in these systems reflects the needs of the business. If not, these new ERP and CRM systems will be the source of frustration and business failures.

Metadata discovery, data profiling, and data reconciliation are all used by reactive organizations as they migrate to cross-functional applications. Business rules monitoring, identity management, and data quality are used in the migration process as well as in maintaining the new CRM systems and ERP systems as they move to production. Let's look at how the metadata analysis, business rules monitoring, and data reconciliation can augment the data profiling, identity management and data quality technology to help reactive organizations make better use of their data.

METADATA ANALYSIS

One financial services company began a data governance campaign with a mandate to do a baseline assessment of all data within their IT infrastructure. Unfortunately, in early meetings, they realized they had 12,000 separate databases within the enterprise that would be included in this analysis. Furthermore, each database had hundreds of tables and thousands of columns. It would have been impossible to do an assessment of all the data, profiling the data alone would have taken years. The best way to approach the problem was to prioritize the assessment and to determine the relationships across different data sources. The only way to accomplish a survey of this much data was through metadata analysis. Only after metadata analysis could a reasonable approach to data profiling, cleansing, and integration begin.

Your organization is constantly accumulating increasing amounts of corporate data. Controlling this data means launching data quality and data integration projects to create a more consistent, accurate, and reliable view of the enterprise. Fortunately, metadata analysis provides a way to get these projects off the ground faster and more reliably.

> Metadata is the data about your corporate data, found in every data source throughout your enterprise.

Metadata is the data about your corporate data, found in every data source throughout your enterprise. It is a crucial part of the data discovery process. Metadata is what describes the information in your data resources. With metadata analysis you get a clear view of these resources—and the most efficient strategy for success with your data quality and data integration initiatives.

Organizations need to understand metadata and its role in keeping data clean and manageable. In reviewing metadata, organizations may find that some applications capture too much data. Or they may have data that is so hard to capture (perhaps the cell phone number of a contact) or changes so frequently that fields are too often blank.

Metadata analysis allows you to gain a clear view of the information contained in your enterprise data resources. Through metadata analysis, you can:

- Organize data logically across all of your data sources: If you have a dozen applications, which ones contain customer data? Which have just product data? Which have a blend of the two?

- Accurately group related data for data management programs: For a customer data improvement program, you may need to logically group data from a disparate network of applications and data sources. Metadata analysis helps you seek out and link those different sources.

- Exclude irrelevant data: Too often, databases contain columns or tables full of inconsequential or spurious data. Metadata analysis helps you understand where good data is and how to bring it into a data management project.

- Organize your data and prioritize data in order to begin more in depth data profiling and data analysis.

Metadata analysis allows you to understand the exact nature of the information in all of your corporate data sources, organize it successfully, and ensure that all of your data quality initiatives run smoothly.

Metadata analysis and data discovery will help you identify and catalog the data throughout your organization. But technical metadata is only one part of the picture. Certainly, it is important to understand the data elements and their relationships to each other. However, it is equally important to understand the business value of those data elements and to build a data dictionary that describes the data sources in a way that business users can understand the nature of the data. There are two parts to the data discovery phase:

- The IT staff is usually responsible for documenting and cataloging the technical metadata.

- The business experts should then use this rich catalog of information to add business metadata. Business metadata includes things like:
  - Who is responsible for this data?
  - How was this data captured?
  - If any calculations are part of this data, what are the calculations? If the data is an amalgamation of data from other sources, what are those sources, and how was the data compiled?

Business metadata is essential for helping organizations understand the meaning of the data within the context of their business processes.

The key to metadata analysis is understanding and organizing metadata from anywhere in the enterprise. Metadata analysis provides the ability to analyze your metadata from existing data sources throughout the enterprise, providing the foundation for more precise data profiling and data quality efforts. Because it provides an understanding of what data you have—and which sources have what type of information—metadata analysis can be essential to building a road map for data management.

BUSINESS RULES

To provide consistency of applications across lines of business, companies need data quality tools to perform more in-depth examinations of data in the form of business rules monitoring capabilities that help organizations establish and enforce complex, configurable standards for data.

By creating and monitoring consistent business rules, you can:

- Enforce data governance standards.
- Audit and validate the quality of your company's data on an ongoing basis.
- Create customized rules to streamline your operational processes.
- Identify and fix operational inefficiencies with a continual, automated enforcement of preset rules.
- Improve the accuracy of your business processes.
- Understand and refine those processes by logging exceptions and violations to business rules in a repository, allowing you to see and address trends.

Business rules technology must be jointly implemented by business and IT. The business analysts create the rules, and IT deploys them for any data-driven initiative. These business rules include detecting unexpected variances, validating numeric calculations, testing domain values against a list of acceptable values, or validating data before allowing a transaction to continue.

Once you discover violations, data-monitoring software automatically notifies designated users of rule violations. The technology can automatically correct the data or copy the violated data to a repository for further examination and correction. The ability to create a number of different outcomes (write to a file, create an alert, start a corrective routine, and so forth) is extremely powerful, because it gives you the flexibility to create complex business rules to manage virtually any situation.

With these capabilities, the business rules engine becomes a tool to ensure that data meets organizational standards. These rules then become a critical control mechanism within data governance or operational compliance efforts.

WHAT IS A BUSINESS RULE?

Are you asking yourself, "What is a business rule, and how is that different from any data rule?" A clear difference of a business rule versus a technical data rule can be seen in an example from the health care industry. In a health care database a technical data rule might exist establishing that a patient must be "Male" or "Female" and that a patient might be "Pregnant" or "Not Pregnant." "Male/Female" and "Pregnant/Not Pregnant" can be validated with simple technical metadata rules to ensure the files adhere to the predefined valid values. However, the database could contain valid values for "Gender" and "Pregnant" fields and a database record might have a combination of "Male" and "Pregnant." This is perfectly valid from a technical metadata perspective. Obviously, the existence of a pregnant male in a database shows an error in the data, even though the diagnosis and gender are both valid entries in the database. It is the relationship between the two that is in violation. The combination of "Male" and "Pregnant" violates a basic business rule industry. No matter

(Continued)

how complex or proprietary the rule is, you can establish a control mechanism to ensure that incoming data meets it. For any company attempting to gain more control over enterprise data, business rule creation and business rule monitoring can report the changing nature of corporate information over time. A critical aspect of a data quality initiative is to help all members of the organization—from executives to line employees—understand the validity of the data.

DATA RECONCILIATION

Imperative to the success of the reactive organization is the ability to bring together departments, divisions, or lines of business. This is often performed via implementations of ERP applications, CRM systems, or data warehouses. Central to these implantations is the ability to understand and resolve duplicate information across sources. This technology allows you to reduce the confusion caused by a single customer, product, or other entity being represented by multiple records. You can also use linking and matching to understand product and item characteristics from different databases or applications. Data reconciliation technology helps you identify these records and determine which data survives as the best attributes for the linked records. This data survivorship will select the most appropriate way to represent the entity in your new systems.

FINDING DUPLICATE CUSTOMER RECORDS

Data reconciliation technologies identify hidden relationships buried deep within your data stores. By using identity resolution and matching technology you can consolidate information, enabling you to build one single, unified view of your data.

Whether you need a solution to identify duplicate records, link customers into households or products to product families, uncover fraudulent activities, or link information across multiple data sources, data

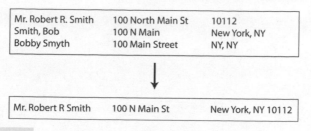

Mr. Robert R. Smith	100 North Main St	10112
Smith, Bob	100 N Main	New York, NY
Bobby Smyth	100 Main Street	NY, NY

| Mr. Robert R Smith | 100 N Main St | New York, NY 10112 |

FIGURE 14.1 **Through data matching, customer data can be consistent and accurate**

reconciliations provide matching and data survivorship that can help you transform raw data into intelligent information (see Figure 14.1).

In this example, you have to build better customer information across every data source within your enterprise. Data reconciliation technology uses logic and problem-solving methods similar to those used by humans. The technology provides the ability to reconcile pattern and formatting differences, phonetic, and spelling errors. This helps the technology understand, for example, that "Robert," "Bobby," and "Bob" are derivatives of the same name or that "100 Main," "100 North Main," and "100 Main St." are potentially the same address. With this prebuilt intelligence, reconciliation technology can identify and consolidate duplicates with unparalleled accuracy and performance.

Poor data integration and reconciliation can jeopardize ERP, CRM, data warehousing, business intelligence, or any other initiative that relies on accurate data drawn from multiple sources. An effective data integration strategy can lower costs and improve productivity by ensuring the consistency, accuracy, and reliability of data across your enterprise. Data integration enables you to:

- Match, link, and consolidate multiple data sources together to create the best possible view of a customer, product, supplier, employee, asset or other data.

- Gain access to the right data sources at the right time to facilitate data integration and spur enhanced decision making.

- Ensure that high-quality information arrives at new data targets during data migration or consolidation efforts.

- Access and reconcile your data on any platform during an integration project.
- Improve the quality of your business information before loading it into new systems.

In the reactive stage, organizations are taking the first step toward integrating their corporate data. By building on data profiling, data quality, and identity management with technologies for metadata analysis, data reconciliation and shared business rules, the reactive organization is beginning to integrate across lines of business and functional areas. This is a critical step toward a governed organization. As I have said, the path to a governed organization must be taken one step at a time, and this is an essential step. Remember that the reactive organization thinks globally, although it acts locally. Learning from these initiatives as a reactive organization is critical. You learn:

- How to get people to work together in defining the organization.
- Which technology is useful in building and managing quality data.
- The state of your systems, applications, and data and the readiness of these systems to be integrated.

The consolidation of lines of business and functional areas is a necessary step for all organizations to make. With the lessons learned from these initiatives, you are ready to begin the move to a proactive organization to consolidate even larger parts of your organization.

CHAPTER 15

Proactive Organizations: Bridging the Chasm and Becoming Proactive

We cannot cross that bridge until we come to it, but I always like to lay down a pontoon ahead of time.

—BERNARD BARUCH

EXECUTIVE OVERVIEW

The move to the proactive stage is the hardest transition for a company to make. Reactive organizations, after all, still have a number of informational silos such as enterprise resource planning (ERP), customer relationship management (CRM), and other enterprise applications that manage a functional area.

In this chapter, organizations will learn how to start viewing data as a shared resource. This is an important step to start profiting from master data management (MDM) technologies designed around domain-specific groups such as customers, products, suppliers, or assets. Reaching this stage requires diplomacy and leadership skills to push back on those who are more comfortable with information silos.

(continued)

(Continued)

This chapter will review several critical integration steps for proactive organizations that are necessary: domain data models, business data services, data delivery and business user interfaces, utilizing data services, data steward tools, and data federation and data synchronization technologies. These technologies need to be integrated into the proactive organization.

REMEMBER

1. Data quality and data governance should *never* be considered a one-time project. A quality culture must be established as an ongoing, continuous process.

2. No organization can tackle enterprise-wide data quality and data governance all at once. To be successful, your journey must be evolutionary. Start small and take achievable steps that can be measured along the way.

How do you get to be one of only 10 to 15 percent of companies who have matured to the proactive stage in the Data Governance Maturity Model? I wish it was as easy as sharing one secret, telling you that you need one technology, or arguing that hiring the brightest CIO is all you need. But organizations typically evolve through a potentially wrenching culture shift. As discussed in Part Three, proactive organizations treat data as a corporate asset, have executive sponsorship, and involve business users in critical decisions. Proactive organizations are beyond the stage of arguing over the usability of their data and have fully-developed customer relationship management (CRM), enterprise resource planning (ERP), and other enterprise applications.

It is one thing, however, to have functioning CRM or ERP systems. It is another to reach that next step of using data from all of these applications to build an enterprise-wide picture of customers, products, employees, or finances. This is the grail of any organization—that the data on a customer in one department or business unit perfectly matches the information viewed by another business unit.

Master Data Management: The Foundation of the Proactive Organization

The proactive organization begins using master data management (MDM) technologies to look specifically at a data type such as customer, product, employee, supplier, or asset. A financial or retail company might initially centralize the data around customers. Manufacturers or distributors might first centralize data around the product.

I am a firm believer in the step approach to MDM. If you try to do an enterprise-wide MDM and try to do it all at once, you will face a long, complicated, and, ultimately, unsuccessful effort. You are going to lose the confidence of executives, and ultimately, lose the funding. Creating a unified view of all assets is simply too complex for an organization as a starting point.

Yet your organization cannot rely, long-term, on the enterprise applications themselves. These solutions cannot answer the tough questions that many companies face. Take the company that has noticed that it is losing customers. The question is why. A database marketing solution tells you that more customers are asking to be removed from e-mail and mailing lists. Your CRM system might tell you about the age or income of these customers. A data warehouse can show trends in buying behavior. The reason behind the customer churn is not contained in any one of these systems but in the sum of information from all the systems. Knowing customer buying behavior and linking it to your marketing initiatives is imperative. Knowing what different demographic groups are buying and linking this information to the applications that drive the day-to-day customer relationships is necessary for success.

You cannot answer the questions about customer churn unless you pull together information from all your applications. For example, consider a large banking institution. Customers are closing out deposits or not renewing certificates of deposit (CDs). The CRM solution might tell you that some of these are high-income customers who are not renewing CDs because it would put them over the FDIC insurance limit on deposits. That makes sense, but there are other high-income clients who continue to remain under the FDIC cap, and they are pulling money out also. At this point you need to look deeper — maybe over in the loan processing office. Financial turmoil has caused the loan office to pull in the reins on lending. Or, by matching up the data from the different systems, you could discover that high-income depositors are pulling their accounts after their home equity line is not renewed or their small business loan was rejected. This is the kind of question that an MDM solution can answer.

According to Gartner:

> Many enterprises are overwhelmed with data, and they spend a lot of money trying to integrate, organize, fact check and otherwise manage it. This leads to data redundancy and the lack of a single view, which damages an enterprise's capability to make effective business decisions. However, most enterprise leaders don't realize that, beyond these obvious costs and the lack of a single view of semantically clean and persistent master data, the business also wastes opportunities to increase revenue and profits, reduce time to market, become more efficient, improve customer service, and reduce business and IT complexity. The lack of "a single version of the truth" regarding data probably won't drive an enterprise out of business; ultimately, however, it will hurt competitiveness and insidiously add to IT and business costs.
>
> The answer isn't more integration, more business intelligence (BI), or more metadata—it's MDM, which amounts to a new way of dealing with data.[1]

It is important to note that this is not a move that IT undertakes independently. That is why a proactive organization stresses that technology changes are driven by business issues. The line of business sets the objectives; IT carries them out. In this stage of the Data Governance Maturity Model, IT is a facilitator helping to find, purchase, install, and maintain the technology that lets business users ask questions like "Why am I losing customers?" At this stage, IT understands the need to have a quality data layer sitting on top of time-tested discrete applications to allow a holistic view of the customer or the product. All the technology that is in use is to support a culture of data quality and transparency.

Domain-specific MDM looks at the applications that gather, maintain, and utilize similar data—like customer or product data. It goes without saying that businesses should start with the data domain that is most important to them. The business should start with a domain that solves an immediate and well articulated business problem. For example:

- A financial services, telecommunications, entertainment, or retail organization will focus on building MDM for customer data to help facilitate up-sell and cross-sell to the customer base.

- A manufacturer may initially build on product MDM to optimize the supply chain cost and delivery.

- A pharmaceutical company may want to concentrate on physician MDM to get a better understanding for the relationships they have with different doctors and health care professionals.

At this point you may be thinking, *Don't manufacturers have customers and retailers buy products?* Obviously they do. A proactive organization focuses on delivering the maximum benefit possible from the initial MDM efforts, regardless of what data they are evaluating. And, as you plan, you need to think globally about how things ultimately piece together. You cannot realistically do it all at once, so you make sure you plan for all the domains and lines of business and implement them as the business dictates. MDM is not so much an expensive undertaking as it is a time-consuming one. Breaking the project into manageable pieces and using the success of one piece to convey the need for going toward the full MDM approach just makes more sense.

The proactive organization facing any kind of regulatory requirement is also likely to look at a cross-enterprise approach toward data governance to support compliance. There is a tendency to view regulatory compliance as discrete and unconnected to the organization. Here are two arguments for a more proactive approach to data for industries that face high regulatory hurdles.

Although it may seem to be a logical next step, the move to the proactive stage is the hardest transition for a company to make. The reason is due to the different philosophies that govern organizations in these two stages. A reactive organization still has a number of informational silos—ERP, CRM, and other enterprise applications that manage a functional area. These silos can be pretty broad, but the organization still has data on customers or products spread out in a variety of disconnected applications.

A proactive organization, however, is beginning to view data as a shared resource. The data collected by the marketing

(Continued)

department is just as valuable to—and should be shared with—the accounts payable department. While this seems like an innocuous shift, it can be a tricky transition, fraught with opportunities for mistakes, delays, and even in-fighting.

The reason: Data, or any information, is a powerful thing. And the control of that resource is not something any business unit will relinquish easily. The chasm represents the complexity of this change. The change is not just a shift in technology. It is a fundamental change in the culture of an organization.

FIGURE 15.1   The Chasm

In light of "know your customer" and anti-terrorism legislation, most financial institutions require applications that flag questionable accounts as they are opened. That information can be gained from one discrete application, even if it is disconnected from other applications. But for other high-risk areas—such as electronic fund transfers or parking money in cash value life insurance policies—the information in these transactions often comes from multiple systems. Your organization needs to be able to look for and flag suspicious activity in many business units and draw connections between the activities. This requires a customer MDM environment that is integrated into all touch points across the organization.

Another critical reason for consolidating information across applications is to create business rules for the entire enterprise like the mortgage reseller that was struggling to get consistency in loan assessment. A loan considered too risky to buy by one unit was approved by another. This organization could not ascertain its overall risk. This is not to say that each unit must be treated exactly the same. The reseller just needed one uniform way to judge the risk of its entire portfolio on any given day and manage the risk across the enterprise. This required a mortgage master data architecture that developed rules centrally and propagated those rules across all lines of business. Based on lessons learned in the subprime mortgage crisis and the resulting financial difficulties, companies need both to *develop* and *enforce* rules to assess risk—and perform these checks across the enterprise.

Although the guiding principles of a proactive organization may seem to be a departure from standard business procedures, reaching data maturity does not involve retiring old applications and starting fresh. At this point, the proactive organization has a particularly robust data quality and integration layer that sits on top of these applications. The rules that govern these organizations are managed by data stewards from business units. The proactive organization has firm definitions for everything from how to define a customer to how to define the raw materials that go into a product. The data in these individual applications comes from a single repository that is propagated across the IT infrastructure. This provides the ultimate in control for the enterprise; because all data, reports, and dashboards draw from the same pool of information.

Even if the proactive organization has taken all the initial steps, the organization still has its work cut out for it. Essential to the successful development of the MDM are various technologies that will facilitate the MDM effort. As an organization moves to the proactive stage, efforts need to be made to integrate several key components:

- **Domain data models.** The domain data models encapsulate the data elements that were decided on by the business experts, in conjunction with the data stewards and IT professionals. These reflect your business as represented in the data. Most MDM vendors have preliminary data models that can be used to get you started—of course, you'll have to optimize them to completely reflect your organization.

- **Business data services.** Fundamental to the success of your MDM system is your ability to have the data reflected in the various applications and business processes that run your organization. Data services are technology work flows that do just that. They surface the data in your MDM environment into your operational and analytical systems. Enhancing business data services for process automation is covered more completely in Chapter 9. Data services are the language of the service-oriented architecture. While MDM maintains the data that reflects your organization, it is the business services that make the data universally available.

- **Data delivery and business users interfaces.** Your data is no good unless it can be surfaced to the business users across your organization. Data delivery technologies surface the data in the format that is required by your business users.

- **Data steward control.** Over time, your business changes. Your MDM system must be flexible enough to allow for these business changes. Data stewards will need to be able to change your MDM system, your business processes, and your data delivery process to reflect the business changes that are required.

- **Data federation technology and data synchronization technology.** It is unreasonable to think that all of your applications and operational systems will be changed to use an MDM data model. Most packaged applications have defined data models that are inflexible. Data synchronization technology will update your applications to reflect the changes to your MDM system. Data federation technologies will be used to access data from across systems without having to modify those systems. These technologies apply business and data rules to data as it is retrieved, before it is passed to the user of other applications.

SERVICE-ORIENTED ARCHITECTURE AND BUSINESS DATA SERVICES

MDM defines, manages, and maintains the data that is the best representation of your organization. Service-oriented architecture (SOA) and data services make the data accessible. Inaccurate data that has entered an enterprise application cannot be easily corrected downstream. Applications may have very unique data structures that have few commonalities with other applications. Extracting this data at a later date and doing batch cleanup and integration can be costly, and it does little to solve the day-to-day problems caused by poor-quality data. Because of this, a layer of prevention is the better approach. Poor-quality data is not caused by a single cataclysmic event; rather, it is the result of ongoing failures in data entry standards, data migration practices, or data collection procedures. What an organization needs is consistency: consistency of data entry, consistency of data validation, consistency across applications. SOA technology enables data management consistency by encapsulating rules and validation techniques into services that can be extended across the enterprise.

For example, product classification can be challenging. In a manufacturing company there may be hundreds of materials from dozens of suppliers under a search table within an ERP system. Faced with this daunting task, most employees have devised shortcuts for product classifications that allow them to complete the job more quickly. Other employees may use different classifications for the same product. This inconsistency can drastically affect ordering new materials and skew the manufacturer's ability to negotiate with suppliers. A data service will ensure that the employee has to choose from a consistent, approved set of classifications. And this service can be implemented in all systems that do product classification.

In this scenario, a data quality system can integrate with the ERP system and other systems that perform product classification for materials to improve the business process—in this case, finding the right product within the system. The data quality technology would match product descriptions to a product classification system. With this system in place, all products would have a standard code and an associated hierarchy of information about them. Using the data service, the rules and validation techniques would be kept independently of any particular application but could be applied to all applications (ERP, CRM, proprietary, data warehouse, and so on). With more uniform product information, the organization can find parts faster—and then do more accurate spend analysis and supply chain optimization in the future.

Master data management does not happen all at once. It is an iterative process that focuses on building consistent data across lines of business—based on the most pressing needs of the organization. Take manageable steps in implementing MDM. Accomplish your initial goals, show the return on investment to your executive sponsors, and then tackle the next business problem. Each business problem will expand the reach of the domain or, eventually, evolve to incorporate other domains. You will be well on your way to becoming a governed organization.

■ **NOTE**

1. Gartner Inc. (Andrew White, John Radcliffe, Chad Eschinger), "Predictions 2009: Master Data Management Is Applicable in Down Economies and in Times of Growth," by Andrew White, et al. December 19, 2008.

CHAPTER 16

Governed Organizations: Moving Beyond Data to Business Process Automation

The man who removes a mountain begins by carrying away small stones.

—WILLIAM FAULKNER

EXECUTIVE OVERVIEW

Governed organizations are rare breeds. Nonetheless, they have a few things in common. They trust their data, and that trust allows them to confidently automate many processes. Governed organizations are way ahead of the competition in compliance, customer relations, and operational efficiency.

This chapter explains that the key difference between proactive and governed organizations is in two major technology areas:

- Multidomain master data management
- Business process automation

The interesting thing about reaching this stage is that the proactive organization has already done the groundwork to move to the governed stage. From a technology standpoint, the next step chiefly involves further
(continued)

(Continued)

integration and cross-functional solutions. But the really hard work, the culture shift and behavioral shift, was necessary in moving to proactive.

REMEMBER

1. Data quality and data governance should *never* be considered a one-time project. A quality culture must be established as an ongoing, continuous process.

2. No organization can tackle enterprise-wide data quality and data governance all at once. To be successful, your journey must be evolutionary. Start small and take achievable steps that can be measured along the way.

Governed organizations trust their data. They have spent time and resources on creating a reliable repository of information that can support both long-term strategic decisions and day-to-day activities. Not only do these organizations trust the data, they also trust that the business side is the one that should be in charge of all data-driven projects. This is not to diminish the role of IT, because in the governed organization, IT is a partner with business in deploying technology that helps the business improve decision making and better run the organization.

Governed organizations make compliance, customer relations, and operational efficiency a high priority. The silo-driven applications of individual business units cannot give organizations satisfactory answers on these topics. A governed organization, through its cohesive view of information, can excel in each of these areas.

BUSINESS BENEFITS OF BECOMING A GOVERNED ORGANIZATION

Let's look at compliance again. By definition, compliance is looking at different parts of your organization without integrated applications and rationalizing information from across your organization to prove compliance. We have seen time and time again that organizations will say they are in compliance. Then, auditors come in and say, "Your report indicates you are in compliance; now, prove that your report is accurate." In that case, organizations just throw up their hands because there is no cohesion of data, which makes it almost impossible to reproduce the reports with any precision.

The same applies to customer relations and revenue generation. A critical component to any customer retention program is ensuring the data in your call center, database marketing system, or financial systems is reliable. Governed organizations have gone through the pain of defining customers, modeling relationships, and creating a shared repository of information via master data management (MDM). They have the tools and experience to create more effective, profitable relationships with customers, providing an impressive competitive advantage.

Operational efficiency is also difficult to manage without maximizing data across multiple applications and touch points. Part One highlighted the experience of an $8 billion company that was rationalizing indirect spend, something defined as all the things they bought that didn't actually go into the products they made; items such as computers, paper, and desks. However, in their procurement system, a curved desk and a black desk and a round desk were all different things until they used technology to rationalize the spend data. Then, they were able to see the total number of desks that they purchased. They also uncovered new and surprising trends about buying patterns which allowed them to approach suppliers with contract requirements and to save money. A combination of data quality and matching technologies, along with good data management techniques, allowed them to reach their goal. The return on investment (ROI) they were seeking came within months, not years, helping the company gain executive buy-in for further data governance efforts.

I have talked repeatedly about reaching a stage where your data is clean enough and organized enough that you can automate some of your business processes. The less manual intervention your organization needs the better. Let's look at what is driving MDM applications and why it is important to make the leap from domain-specific MDM to enterprise-wide MDM. If you are a retailer and your customer data-focused MDM can tell you everything about red sweater sales in December in the Upper Midwest, you may not see the value of incorporating buyers and suppliers into the MDM equation. Just as long as you communicate the demand for red sweaters to the vendors in some sort of timely fashion, you are covered. Right? Maybe not. What if your buyers know on a day-to-day basis how many red sweaters you are selling and how that compares to previous years? From that information, orders could be adjusted automatically, upwards if red sweaters are flying off the shelves or downward, so the retailer has fewer red sweaters to offload to the outlet store come May. This type of insight requires you to manage customer trends data together with historic product sales data.

Here is another example. A telecommunications company has a customer  MDM system, integrating information from sales, marketing, their Web site and the call center. The company has recently introduced a new high-end cable box to support high-definition cable and digital recording capabilities. All customer data flows into an MDM hub. It indicates that the company is losing customers at a slightly higher rate than before. With their customer MDM, they might even be able to tie the losses to within a month of a service call related to a cable box. But is the information about the type of cable box this customer received as well as call center and repair information about that particular model recorded with the customer data? And can any of that be easily shared with the group responsible for buying the boxes from a vendor. How long would it take, and how many customers would you lose, before you figure out your organization possibly bought a bad batch of boxes, or simply bought a unit that is not customer-friendly? Only by integrating product and supplier information into the MDM system can the company begin to understand the answers to these questions.

Governing your data is more than an exercise of straightening up the company files. It really is about being able to move rapidly against the competition, seize market share, reduce costs, control the risk of regulatory fines, and make your shareholders happy. In economically difficult times, striving for this goal is not a luxury, it is a necessity.

The Path to Governed

Getting to the governed stage is not something that happens overnight. It is a gradual evolution. Certain departments, lines of business, applications, or domains will become governed before others. From a technology perspective, you become a governed organization by continuing to enhance what you accomplished as a proactive organization. This is particularly true in two major technology areas:

1. Multidomain master data management.
2. Business process automation.

During the period as a proactive organization, continuous additions are made to the master data management system. Additional lines or businesses are incorporated, forcing the proactive organization to continue to add to the domain data model and to eventually incorporate additional domains. Eventually, all critical aspects of the business will be incorporated into the data model. There will be one, and only one, representation of corporate data that truly reflects the entire business.

But, as I have said before, managing data for the sake of data is not a productive use of your organization's resources. You manage data to improve the business. I started this book by asserting that data needed to be treated as corporate asset, to be funded as a corporate asset and to be managed as a corporate asset. Like anything that an organization funds, there is an expectation that there will be a return on that investment. The return on data management and data governance investments becomes most pronounced when it is used to:

- Automate and optimize business processes.
- Automate and optimize business decision making.

Using Technology to Move Along the Governance Path

Substantial technologies are needed to make this happen, but almost all of the technologies to move from proactive to governed are in the areas of integration. In this particular case, the integration is into business processes that drive your day-to-day operations and your strategic decision making. Some of this may be implemented by utilizing service-oriented architecture (SOA) to drive services into your business applications and decision support systems. But often the interfaces to these environments are proprietary and may not be conducive to SOA. In these cases, you must develop specific data services that will optimize and automate the proprietary business processes—based on the data in your MDM system. Think about all the systems in your organization that have customer data: your sales force automation system, your marketing databases, your financial systems, your distribution systems, and your customer data warehouse. What happens today if an existing call center customer creates a new profile on your Web site? Chances are, a new customer record is created. This customer already exists in many of your other systems. In this case, a duplicate customer record is created and eventually propagated throughout all of your IT systems. This is how customer service, financial analysis, and many other aspects of your business begin to erode. Automation of data services into business processes creates one, and only one, way of determining if a customer exists. All applications—from finance to marketing to sales to distribution to your Web site—should use the same data service to check for existence of a customer. This ensures that your data reflects your organization and provides a truly governed data environment.

The ability to become a governed organization is built on the successes of the proactive organization. The evolution to business-driven decisions in IT and the painstaking evolution to cooperative approaches have already taken place. The technologies that will make for a successful governed organization are the combination of MDM and SOA—MDM to make sure your data reflects your organization and SOA to ensure that this corporately correct data is consistently pushed into your business processes.

The economic climate has been challenging recently, to say the least. It may seem that reaching governed status is a low priority when faced with decisions about layoffs, shuttering a unit, or discontinuing a product line. Governed organizations can make these difficult decisions much more effectively. If a company has not reached this level, it risks eliminating the wrong products, alienating its best customers, or downsizing their most critical employees—potentially fatally hampering their ability to take advantage of economic recovery. If you take away nothing else from this book, remember that data governance and data quality are critical to making the right decisions for your organization, the kind of decisions that will help your organization prosper well into the twenty-first century.

CONCLUSION

I started this book with a quote from Aristotle, "The whole is more than the sum of its parts." As you get started on your path to becoming a governed organization, it is important to remember what you are trying to accomplish. Your data is one of the few proprietary assets that you have available. As such, your data should reflect the whole of your organization. Your goal is to improve your organization, one step at a time. As you make improvements in your data management processes, you will quickly notice incremental improvements in your organization. And as the different aspects of your organization work toward the same goals—built on a consistent infrastructure of data—you will realize that the whole is more than the sum of the parts.

But don't try to do it all at once. The key points to remember are:

- **Any improvement in your processes needs to be based on a solid business case.** Start with the areas that will yield the most benefit to your organization and tackle the issues one at a time. To be successful, you have to have executive sponsorship and support. To get this support, identify the benefits to your business.

- **Understand the capacity of your organization.** Take the time to assess where your organization falls within the Data Governance Maturity Model. With this assessment, you will understand the process, people and technology changes that need to be implemented for *your* organization. All businesses and organizations are different. Understand your organization so you will know how to make the most effective changes.

- **Embrace the quality culture.** Ultimately, it is only through a culture shift throughout your organization that you will be successful. The quality culture is a change in the way you approach all aspects of your business. Get people involved by demonstrating the way a culture of quality will lead to a quality organization.

- **Define a data management methodology that works for you.** This needs to be a repeatable process, one that is embraced for all applications and all lines of business. Your methodology may be similar to the one defined in this book, or it may not. Find what works for you.

- **Technology is an enabler for your organization.** But technology alone will not solve your problems. Embrace the technologies that will help you make the incremental changes in your organization—but do it in conjunction with the policy and personnel changes that are needed to make you successful.

Data governance and organizational quality data require a long journey. It is a trip that has to be taken one step at a time. But, with every step comes additional benefits for your organization. Remember: You cannot do this all at once. But the sooner you get started, the sooner you will reap the benefits. Start now, build the quality culture into your organization, and ensure the long term viability and success of your business.

Glossary

analytical systems The technology used for business intelligence and decision support. Analytical systems allow companies to access and present information to help them make better decisions for operational as well as strategic execution.

B2B Business to business.

B2C Business to consumer.

Basel II A set of regulations that aims to improve the consistency of international capital regulations, make regulatory capital more risk-sensitive and forward-looking, and promote enhanced risk-management practices. Basel II encourages financial institutions to identify risks they may face to develop improved methods of managing those risks.

business experts Individuals that understand the business processes, decisions, and rules that dictate the way their functional areas operate. Business experts play a pivotal role by using their expertise to help the data governance committee craft the appropriate data definitions and rules. They ensure that the data models, the data rules, and the data usage are fit-for-purpose for the needs of their line of business.

business intelligence Skills and technologies used to help organizations make better decisions by better understanding their business, their market, and their customers.

business process The defined method for a range of activities that organizations perform. A business process can include anything from the steps needed to make a product to how a supply is ordered or how an invoice is created.

business rules The defined operations and constraints that help organizations create a data environment that promotes efficient operations and decision making. An example of a business rule for a hospital would be that no male patient can be marked pregnant. Organizations typically have thousands of business rules, but not all facets of the same organizations follow all of them—and, in some cases, the rules can conflict.

customer relationship management (CRM) The technology and processes used to capture the details of interactions with customers and analyze that data to improve customer interaction, assess customer value, and build value and further loyalty.

dashboard   A means of providing information in a straightforward way. Like the part in a car it is named after, a business dashboard allows executives to see key metrics about anything from monthly sales to manufacturing downtime.

data attributes   A characteristic of a data element, such as whether it is numeric or character, follows a specific pattern, can or cannot be null, or has to be unique.

data cleansing   The process of reviewing and improving data to make sure it is correct, up to date, and not duplicated.

data consolidation   The process of combining data from numerous silos, databases, platforms, applications, and technologies into fewer databases, applications, and platforms.

data federation   Technology that joins data from different sources, operational or analytic, around an organization. Data federation allows users to have a single view of disparate data without having to understand the details of the individual data sources.

data governance   The process for addressing how data enters the organization, who is accountable for it, and how—using people, processes, and technologies—data achieves a quality standard that allows for complete transparency within an organization.

data governance council   An internal committee of interdepartmental members that set data policies, processes, and standards for the organization.

data integration   The process of coherently using data from across platforms, applications or business units. Data integration ensures that data from different sources is merged allowing silos of data to be combined.

data management   The policies, procedures, and technologies that dictate the granular management of data in an organization. This includes supervising the quality of data and ensuring it is used and deployed properly.

data management lifecycle   A repeatable process to manage, monitor, and maintain data.

data migration   The process of migrating data to or from an application such as moving data from a sales force automation tool to a data warehouse.

data model   A means of encapsulating the data elements that were decided on by the business experts, in conjunction with the data stewards and IT professionals. The data models reflect an organization's business as represented in the data

data profiling   A process for looking at the data within the source systems and understanding the data elements and the anomalies. A thorough data profiling exercise alerts organizations to data that does not meet the characteristics defined in the metadata compiled during data exploration. Data profiling also identifies whether data meets business needs and can determine relationships across data sources.

data service   Any function call, business object, or query that can be executed as an encapsulated logic block. The benefit of data services is that they can be written once and executed by many different applications. Data services can be very granular, for instance, "What is the customer address?" Alternatively, data services can represent larger units of work, for instance, "Does this customer already exist in our company?" Multiple applications can execute the same data service providing consistency of processes.

data steward   Critical players in data governance councils. Comfortable with technology and business problems, data stewards seek to speak up for their business units when an organization-wide decision will not work for that business unit. Yet they are not turf protectors, instead seeking solutions that will work across an organization. Data stewards are responsible for communication between the business users and the IT community.

data transformation   Converting data from one format to another—making the data reflect the needs of the target application. Used in almost any data initiative, for instance, a data service or an ETL (extract, transform, load) process.

data quality   This term refers to whether an organization's data is reliable, consistent, up to date, free of duplication, and can be used efficiently across the organization.

data warehouse   A technology platform that stores business data for analysis and strategic decision-making purposes. Data warehouses gather information from across the organization and typically maintain historical data across lines of business.

enterprise resource planning (ERP)   An information system that coordinates resources that are needed to perform business functions such as order fulfillment and billing.

executive sponsor   A C-level executive engaged in data governance and the process of achieving that goal.

extract, transform, load (ETL)   A workflow process used when transferring data from one system to another, specifically moving data to a data warehouse. Typically used to describe the process of acquiring source system data, manipulating it based on the data and business rules and then populating a data warehouse.

identity resolution   Is John Q. Smith the same as John Quincy Smith? Using various attributes and data identity resolution techniques, companies can purge their files of multiple versions of the same customer or the same product listed under multiple names. Identity resolution goes beyond matching in that it will look at a series of attributes (phone number, identifying number) to test for similarities. *Identity resolution* does not just refer to identifying and processing data on people or organizations, but the techniques are equally appropriate for product or other types of data.

information technology (IT)   The department and applications that focus on the development and deployment of technology solutions for the organization.

IT expert   IT experts are the application owners, information architects, and systems analysts that make sure technology requirements are met and documented and incorporated into the overall technology infrastructure.

master data   Data that describes the important details of a business subject area such as customer, product, or material across the organization. Master data allows different applications and lines of business to use the same definitions and data regarding the subject area. Master data gives an accurate, 360° degree view of the business subject.

master data management (MDM)   The guiding principles and technology for maintaining data in a manner that can be shared across various systems and departments throughout an organization.

metadata   Data about the organization's data, found in every data source throughout the enterprise. Metadata describes the information in these data resources. Metadata can be technical, describing the physical characteristics of the data, or it can be business-oriented, describing the way the data represents the needs of the business.

operational systems   The IT systems that run the business on a day-to-day basis. Operational systems maintain transactional data that detail the events of an organization. Data analysis is typically done outside the operational system.

risk management   The process organizations employ to reduce different types of risks. A company manages risk to avoid losing money, protect against breaking government or regulatory body rules, or even assure that adverse weather does not interrupt the supply chain.

Sarbanes-Oxley   Refers to the 2002 Public Accounting Reform Act that requires greater transparency in the way publically-traded companies in the United States report their revenue and profits.

service-oriented architecture (SOA)   An IT infrastructure that allows disparate applications to exchange data and use consistent processes as they interact with each other. SOA is the foundation architecture for data services.

spend management   The method organizations use to control and optimize the money they spend. It seeks to achieve one view of all spending from sourcing supplies to settling bills—and then look for ways to cut spending or consolidate purchases to achieve greater savings.

supply chain management   The management of business units in the provision of products and services. It spans the movement and storage of raw materials, work-in-process inventory, and finished goods from point-of-origin to point-of-consumption.

watch list compliance   Refers to a list of "watched" people or specifically designated individuals that government authorities have identified as suspect individuals. Watch lists normally designate individuals with potential terrorist, money laundering, narcotics, or other criminal activities. The watch list for the United States is identified in the USA PATRIOT Act—passed by the U.S. Congress following the terrorist attacks of September 11, 2001. Among other rules, the USA PATRIOT Act requires financial organizations to report on financial transactions that could be efforts by terrorist or other criminals to launder money. Although not a part of the PATRIOT Act, the U.S. government also compiles a separate watch list or no-fly list that airlines must comply with.

workflow   A series of granular steps that are put together in proper sequence to execute some bit of logic.

Index